The Power of
Multiplication

CELESTE PEREZ

WESTBOW
PRESS®
A DIVISION OF THOMAS NELSON
& ZONDERVAN

WestBow Press books may be ordered through booksellers or by contacting:

WestBow Press
A Division of Thomas Nelson & Zondervan
1663 Liberty Drive
Bloomington, IN 47403
www.westbowpress.com
844-714-3454

ISBN: 978-1-9736-8799-3 (sc)
ISBN: 978-1-9736-8800-6 (hc)
ISBN: 978-1-9736-8798-6 (e)

Library of Congress Control Number: 2020904459

Print information available on the last page.

WestBow Press rev. date: 03/09/2021

Contents

Acknowledgments

There are many factors on how this book came about, so I will mention a few. I love to read, and I encourage others to do the same. I have a personal library, but that was not always the case.

It all started in the sixth grade. My teacher, Mrs. Barry, would take the time to read to us. She would have all students sit on a rug and make us listen to her reading, for example, *The Adventures of Huckleberry Finn*, *Little House on the Prairie*, and many more. Later she would ask us questions.

Little by little, I saw myself going to the library and checking out books to read. So I'm thankful for Mrs. Barry, and God bless if she is still living. I read somewhere that when children see books around the house or are exposed to them, there is a high probability that those children will become readers and intelligent. At home, we had books around because Dad loved to read. I had always seen him reading a book. He is an intelligent man and very knowledgeable about most subjects.

My past congregation is Fruit of the Vine, Inc. located in Gurabo, Puerto Rico. My first visit was in 2009, but it was not until my first visit with my Apostle Angelica Calveti under the gift of the Spirit that she inspired me to write a book. Later in 2014, Apostle Calveti preached again under the anointment she prophesied that there are writers in the congregation who will write books. Since then, that idea had stayed on my mind.

While fasting for seven nights and seven days in 2015 at

Mount Horeb in Palmer, Massachusetts, I was slow and a little weak on my fifth day, but supernaturally from 12:00 p.m. through 3:00 p.m., my writing hand would not stop. I knew this was from God. It was like a flow of the Spirit of God that I could not stop writing. Several times I would close the notebook, and while praying, God would give me more and more to write about. That is how this book was birthed out. The glory is all first and only to God. After several years, finally my first book was birthed.

Dedication

I dedicate this book to the triune God who is the creator of all things including the power of multiplication.

The Power of Multiplication

For I know the thoughts that I think toward you,
says the Lord, thoughts of peace and not of evil,
to give you a future and a hope.[1]
—Jeremiah 29:11

Since the beginning of times, God had a clear image of how he wanted His children to live. Unfortunately, not only have you and I altered that plan, but the great deceiver, Satan, has also played a part. It was never God's intention for you to be stuck or stagnant. The purpose of this book is to demonstrate that God is the originator of the power of multiplication, and through this power, humans have the power to use it for His glory. Today, there are promises that Christians can tap into through the power of multiplication.

God does not want His people to live all their lives depending only on humankind and/or government assistance. For example, during the Great Depression, the New Deal for the American people was created. According to Purcell, "New Deal programs started in early 1933, with a flurry of activity during Roosevelt's First Hundred Days in office for the purpose to help Americans

---

[1] Unless otherwise noted, all biblical passages referenced are in the New King James Version (Nashville: HarperCollins Christian Publishing, 1982).

in need."[2] Many do not know that the government created these public assistance programs for temporary relief so people would get back on their feet or situated financially and then proceed with their lives.

Poverty is a curse, not a blessing. It is not God's plan that His people, your children, or even your grandchildren follow the same steps into poverty. When God appeared to Moses on Mount Horeb, God specifically told Moses what He wanted to do with the chosen. Exodus 3:8 says, "So I have come down to rescue them from the hand of the Egyptians and to bring them up out of that land into a good and spacious land, a land flowing with milk and honey."

God's promises for His chosen people apply to you and me today. God wants to introduce us to a desirable land where we can see the power of multiplication working in our favor. In addition, this book will emphasize that God is willing to introduce His people to a land where they can sow and reap. There is a blessing with your name on it!

[2] Aaron D. Purcell, *Deal and the Great Depression* (Kent, Ohio: The Kent State University Press, 2014), 5.

Chapter 1

Be Fruitful and Multiply

> Then God blessed them, and God said to them,
> "Be fruitful and multiply; fill the earth and subdue
> it; have dominion over the fish of the sea, over the
> birds of the air, and over every living thing that
> moves on the earth."
> —Genesis 1:28

For some awesomely good reason, God commanded Adam, the first man created, to be fruitful and increase. There is a divine purpose behind this commandment. That is powerful because we see here the Creator, the Father of all things, bestowing a blessing, which means that He gave them a divine favor to become fruitful and increase or multiply. For this reason, we see the first Adam active, moving, and doing God's work.

There are many characters mentioned in Scripture where God blessed them. In the case of Noah and his sons (Genesis 9:1), God gave them the privilege to be fruitful and multiply and to fill the earth after the flood. Sarah became the mother of nations and kings of people (Genesis 17:16). A great nation was birthed out of God's promise to Ishmael (Genesis 17:20).

Look at the promises that God has for us. God told Abraham, "I will bless you, and I will multiply your descendants as the stars of the heaven and as the sand which is on the seashore; and your descendants shall possess the gate of their enemies" (Genesis 22:17).

In the case of Rebekah, Abraham sent his servant Eliezer to find a wife for Isaac. The family of Rebekah, in the process of letting her go with Eliezer, declared a blessing upon her (Genesis 24:60). It is interesting to note that Rebekah came from a pagan family. This is seen when Rachel takes idols from Laban's house (Genesis 31:19).

Even though the blessing came from God, Rebekah coming from a pagan family does not limit God to continue His promises. Moreover, through Isaac, God's promise continues through them as well for their descendants. This is true for Christians today that the inspired word of God can come to fruition because He is not a respecter of persons. God did not forget about Abraham's promises, so He reminded Isaac of the promises seen in Genesis 26:3–4, 24. Other examples are Jabez (1 Chronicles 4:10), Job (Job 42:12), Obed-Edom (1 Chronicles 26:5), and so many more.

To understand this passage, it is ideal to dissect its meaning since "Hebrew is the language through which God chose to reveal himself, create his people, used by Jesus, used by the apostles, and gives an understanding of the Old Testament."[3] For example, Genesis 1:28 starts with "Then God blessed them." The word *blessed* used here in Hebrew is וַיְבָרֶךְ ,(barak), meaning "to praise, to bless, blessed, filled with strength, full, praised, and adored."[4]

The word to *be fruitful* in Hebrew is וּפְרוּ, (pārâ), meaning to bear fruit or to be fruitful. Meanwhile, the word *multiply* in Hebrew is וּרְבוּ, (rābâ), meaning to become numerous, increase, grow up, or become great or powerful. The primitive root word

[3] Chet Roden, *Elementary Biblical Hebrew an Introduction to the Language and Its History* (San Diego: Cognella, 2017), 2–3.
[4] Michael S. Heiser, *The English-Hebrew Reverse Interlinear Old Testament New King James Version* (Bellingham, Wash.: Lexham Press, 2009).

is Rabah. In agreement with Dockrey et al., multiply also means "to head up, make abundant, and increase."[5]

A great example is in Genesis 1:22, "And God blessed them, saying, 'Be fruitful and multiply, and fill the waters in the seas, and let the birds multiply on the earth.'" Another example is in Acts 6:7, "Then the word of God spread, and the number of the disciples multiplied greatly in Jerusalem, and a great many of the priests were obedient to the faith."

God is a God that, since the beginning, has demonstrated to humanity the capacity to create. Moreover, God has demonstrated how a blessing blesses in a mighty way, causing humans to have the power to multiply not only in population but also through the works of their hands.

Adam's first responsibility was to take care of the garden and name all the livestock, beasts of the field, and birds of the air. What a huge responsibility! There was so much work to do in God's kingdom with no suitable helper, so God's productive hands created another wonderful human being, the woman.

Our Father God is a productive being. He is always willing to work for all and especially His people. Since the beginning, this wonderful trait has been present. Genesis 1:2 states, "And the Spirit of God was hovering over the waters." The New American Standard Bible (NASB) version uses *moving*[6] instead of hovering. The Spirit of God has always been in a constant movement, causing or producing motion. That is a great revelation because as humans created in the image of God our Father, there is an intrinsic desire to be in movement and productive. For example, when there is no production, companies collapse. The spiritual realm is no different; if we are not productive in the spiritual realm, we are barren.

---

[5] Karen Dockrey, Johnnie Godwin, and Phyllis Godwin, *The Student Bible Dictionary* (Uhrichsville, Ohio: Barbour Publishing, 2000), 160.

[6] *Holy Bible: New American Standard Bible (NASB)* (LaHabra, Calif.: The Lockman Foundation), 1995. As found in the BibleGateway website.

Our heavenly God always has a plan when He says you must be fruitful and multiply. God was giving humankind the authority to take action to produce, be fruitful, and multiply. It is not something that we human beings should try to negotiate with God or make excuses for not following His commands because it is simple: behind that promise, God glorifies, and there are blessings that follow. The alternative produces negative results with a high probability of a negative impact on our future generations. We have that power delegated from God to produce good results, bear fruits abundantly, or produce abundant growth.

Many Christians are walking with a spiritual blindfold from the enemy, preventing them from seeing this great truth. Many Christians listen more to Satan and are bound by his lies, believing phrases such as "I cannot do it," "I am not able," "I am good at nothing," "This is not my calling," "The ministry is not going anywhere," or "Who is going to listen to me?"

Many are walking like zombies, believing they are not capable of producing anything and carrying a heavy burden of negative "cannot," "are nots," and "will nots." Once the truth is grasped, many Christians will see they have the power to produce and multiply. This is exactly what God wants to do in your life this very moment because, in this crucial hour, He is going to use you with that power He delegated to show the world that He is able to do more for His people. The world needs to see that God is bigger than the one who has dominion in the world, so many will come to Christ. 1 John 4:4 states, "Because He who is in you is greater than he who is in the world."

God birthed the ideology of being fruitful and multiplying. Dictionary.com defines the word *idea* as "any conception existing in the mind as a result of mental understanding, awareness, or activity, thought, conception, or notion, an impression."[7] In other words, God thought of us. Psalm 92:5 states, "O Lord, how

---

[7] Dictionary.com, 2015.

great are your works! Your thoughts are very deep." God has profound thoughts about us. He wants us to seek Him, tap into His extraordinary mind and find out what thoughts and ideas He wants us to obtain. God's ideas are therefore accessible for those who desire to seek Him!

Isaiah 55:8–9 says, "For my thoughts are not your thoughts, nor are your ways my ways, says the Lord. For as the heavens are higher than the earth, so are my ways higher than your ways, and my thoughts than your thoughts." God has thoughts for every believer, but sadly, many are unaware of this. This is confirmed in Micah 4:12," But they do not know the thoughts of the Lord, nor do they understand His counsel; for He will gather them like sheaves to the threshing floor." Ask God what His thoughts are about you. You will be amazed at the good thoughts that He has about you.

Chapter 2

Laziness Is a Sin

A little sleep, a little slumber, A little folding of the hands to sleep—So shall your poverty come on you like a prowler, And your need like an armed man.

—Proverbs 6:10-11

God never planned for His people to be in poor condition. We clearly see how God repeatedly warns the people of Israel to follow His commands. Through obedience to His decree, they will not know what lack, scarcity, or poverty is. We find this truth in Deuteronomy 15:4, "Except when there may be no poor among you; for the Lord will greatly bless you in the land which the Lord your God is giving you to possess as an inheritance." The next verse, 15:5, gives us the disclaimer, "Only if you carefully obey the voice of the Lord your God, to observe with care all these commandments which I command you today."

God later provides more instructions because, unfortunately, many people would go astray, follow other gods, and not follow His commandments. The poor came into existence due to disobedience. God knew this would happen. Therefore, we can say that many became poor in Israel because sin brought poverty.

This demonstrates that a nation can be in poverty because of its own sins.

Israel became accustomed to seeing the poor. Many generations later, we can see Jesus speaking about the poor. Jesus said in John 12:8, "For the poor you have with you always, but me you do not have always." Even in Jesus's times, the poor exist, and through His ministry, Jesus healed many of them. Today, the poor still exist, and as we know, God loves the poor just like the rich, and salvation is available to all.

According to Worldvision.org, "736 million people live in extreme poverty, surviving on less than $1.90 a day."[8] It is a fact: millions, including Christians because of generational curses or other factors such as loss of a job or investments, sickness, or scarcity of goods in such territory, are in poverty today, while others are there because of pure laziness.

The meaning of lazy is "disinclined to work." Lazy people do not like to work. They like to sit around, talk, waste time in selfish pleasures, and wait for others to assist them. Some common names for lazy people are couch potatoes, freeloaders, or slackers. While the word *poverty* means being in a state or condition of having little or no money, goods, or means of support, it is a condition of being poor or underprivileged.

I have never met someone who enjoys being poor, but many Christians feel it is always God's will to be poor. Even more, many Christians learned it is a privilege to be poor and not prosperous. Moreover, when I am speaking about prosperity, I am not talking about money because you can be prosperous in many areas of your life, for instance, your health, employment, grace, or relationships with family, friends, or coworkers.

How does a lazy person become lazy? Proverbs 6:10–11 says, "A little sleep, a little slumber, a little folding of the hands to

---

[8] Andrea Peer, "Global poverty: Facts, FAQs, and how to help," https://www.worldvision.org/sponsorship-news-stories/global-poverty-facts.

sleep—so shall your poverty come on you like a prowler, and your need like an armed man." It all starts with giving more time to the flesh. The flesh wants to sleep more, and you will give it for no reason. There is nothing wrong with sleeping in. I have done this occasionally, and I am glad I did it because my body needed a rest.

I am referring to when your flesh starts getting accustomed to sleeping more than usual that it becomes a fleshly habit. Second, the flesh wants to have more time to slumber. Slumber means to sleep, doze, and drowse, to be in a state of inactivity or negligence. The person who sleeps more for no reason, knowing they have responsibilities to take care of, will eventually lead to a matter of negligence. Negligence caused many people to lose their jobs for arriving to work late, making excuses for not being on time, or not showing up at all.

Another word for lazy is a *sluggard*. Proverbs 20:4 says, "The lazy man will not plow because of winter; he will beg during harvest and have nothing." The result of a lazy person is that they will end with nothing.

Furthermore, the sluggard is constantly craving. Proverbs 13:4 confirms, "The soul of a lazy man desires, and has nothing; but the soul of the diligent shall be made rich." Every choice we make brings about consequences. The same goes for those Christians who decide not to work. They may fool their families or friends, but no one can fool God. When a person decides not to work even though they are capable, they will pay the negative consequences.

There are different types of work. Many women decide to be stay-at-home moms, sometimes considered domestic engineers. A full-time mom is hard work, oftentimes more challenging than a full-time job. If a mom ever decides not to do all her responsibilities, that household will break loose or fall.

The spirit of sluggardness opens the door for the enemy to come in and enter. I have seen many people refuse to get a real job, leading them to become dependent on government assistance. Many tend to lie on their applications to get more assistance and become legitimate liars. They forget that the Bible says not to lie, bringing a curse upon them. Oftentimes those lies would lead to making up other lies to hide the first lie. It is a vicious cycle, with Christians staying at home doing nothing.

Sadly, many become sluggards who crave what others have, which may lead to an open door for the enemy to come in. When someone craves something they do not work for, the results are negative, while the diligent, the ones who work fervently for their desires, are fully satisfied. Why? Because the diligent works. The sluggards always want more. The sluggards always desire what they do not have. The sluggards criticize those who have it going on.

Many sluggards are in that situation because of fear. This reminds me of the parable of the talents found in Matthew 25:14–28. The one given five talents and the one given two were able to multiply their productivity, while the one who received one talent was not able to produce. Verse 24 states, "Then he who had received the one talent came and said, 'Lord, I knew you to be a hard man, reaping where you have not sown, and gathering where you have not scattered seed.'"

Here is why so many Christians are bound by the enemy's lies. Fear can come in several ways, but most likely by a negative thought, hearing the lies of the enemy, or by negative experiences. For the man with the one talent, the fear came through a thought because he was pondering that his master was a hard man. So that alone discouraged this man from working harder.

Fear has paralyzed many Christians not to pursue a career, go back to school, or follow God's instructions to go full time in the ministry. Fear has stopped many Christians from following their dreams and passions and being the persons God has always intended. Fear has hindered so many people from experiencing their full potential.

Fear has opened the doors to so many believers who are stagnant or in a rut. Fear is the opposite of faith, and Hebrews

11:6 says, "But without faith, it is impossible to please Him, for he who comes to God must believe that He is and that He is a rewarder of those who diligently seek Him."

The master replied, "You wicked, lazy servant" (Matthew 25:26). First, the master called the servant wicked. This is important because the revelation here is that laziness is an action of the wicked. Then the master called him lazy. It did not take long for the master to realize he had a lazy one in his group. The master for sure did not want this servant under his leadership because eventually this servant could influence others to do the same. I do not know if you have ever worked with a lazy person, but let me tell you, it is not easy and not fun because eventually, they will do nothing, and you will end up doing their work. A lazy person is like a parasite or leech.

Third, a lazy person is following the concept of *closing of the hands*. This means not laboring, not working at all, not moving as they are supposed to do, or not caring to work. Proverbs 21:25 says, "The desire of the lazy man kills him, for his hands refuse to labor." The person finds excuses not to work, not realizing that this path leads him to poverty and death. The appetite of the lazy is pure rebellion to what God has established here on earth. Work is our portion since Adam and Eve sinned. Proverbs 19:24 says, "A lazy man buries his hand in the bowl, and will not so much as bring it to his mouth again."

This "comically portrays the destructive nature of exaggerated laziness: The sluggard is too lazy to even feed himself."[9] A lazy person is an unproductive person. The enemy knows this, so once this happens, you have allowed poverty to come to your doors like a bandit or robber. The aftermath will be that scarcity will follow like an armed man. This is the work of the enemy, as stated in John 10:10, "The thief comes only to steal and kill and destroy."

---

[9] J. D. Barry et al., *Faithlife Study Bible* (Bellingham: Lexham Press, 2012), Proverbs 19:24.

The enemy, the thief, is presently looking to steal ideas, energy, zeal, passion, and dreams. If the enemy can destroy your passion or dreams, then there is no reason to work for it. The enemy wants to lead you to a path of lack or hopelessness.

Laziness is a temptation that the devil utilizes to keep many Christians chained up in poverty and living in scarcity. Matthew 26:41 says, "Watch and pray so that you will not fall into temptation. The spirit is willing, but the body is weak." A way to beat the temptation and overcome laziness is to pray and keep working.

Jesus fasted for forty days and forty nights; the devil came to tempt him. Matthew 4:8 relates, "Again, the devil took Him up on an exceedingly high mountain, and showed Him all the kingdoms of the world and their glory." Moreover, he said to Him, "All these things I will give you if you will fall down and worship me" (Matthew 4:9).

The devil was offering kingdoms of the world and their glory. In agreement with Ravi Zacharias, "The kingdoms of this world were ultimately neither his nor his to give."[10] Second, the devil was offering kingdoms and their glory that he never worked for or created.

When Adam and Eve sinned, Satan took dominion over the earth. However, when Jesus died on the cross, God gave Jesus authority over heaven and earth. Paul warned the Ephesians that the devil worked as "the prince of the power of the air, the spirit who now works in the sons of disobedience" (Ephesians 2:2). Laziness is a spirit that works in the sons of disobedience.

Laziness is a sin, and it is an easy way not to follow God's commands. The road to salvation is a commitment. Christians must work to keep that relationship with Jesus on a daily basis, to be on fire by living a holy life separated from the worldly things

---

[10] Ravi Zacharias, *I, Isaac, take Thee Rebekah* (Nashville: Thomas Nelson, 2004), 80.

that tempt us. Millions of people have already quit and entered the wide gate, relying on their own understanding; many have ended in a place of sorrow and lamentations. Many Christians are quitting right now, while others are being persistent and diligent in walking through the narrow gate.

Again, the easy way is to sin, follow the crowd, and do things against the Word of God. It is so much easier to follow the works of the flesh and lie. It is easy to follow others' gods, make idols of anything, use the Lord's name in vain, or dishonor one's father and mother. It is not difficult to murder these days or commit adultery or fornicate. Stealing is done effortlessly. It is easy to criticize, gossip, or even speak negatively or say bad words. Lastly, it is not easy to follow God's commands and not live an orderly life. The true matter is that the devil, the ruler of this world, has many Christians spiritually sleeping, and many do not know they are walking through the road that leads to the wide gate.

God always appeared in the garden and checked on Adam and Eve, but after the fall, something was different. Both Adam and Eve were not found easily, like other times. Not that God did not know what had happened, but God appeared in the garden, calling to Adam and Eve, and as we know, they were hiding because of sin. Romans 5:12 says, "Therefore, just as through one man, sin entered the world, and death through sin, and thus death spread to all men, because all sinned."

The hiding was their action after sinning, becoming for them the first process of spiritual and physical death. When we sin, it produces shame, disgrace, and the act of being veiled. Things changed quickly for Adam and Eve. God gave them instructions and said in Genesis 3:17–18, "Cursed is the ground for your sake; in toil you shall eat of it all the days of your life. Both thorns and thistles it shall bring forth for you, and you shall eat the herb of the field."

Oden states, "Who commanded that there come forth so many thorny or poisonous plants that are useless for food and so many trees that bear no fruit?"[11] The thorns and the thistles are a reminder of the cause of sin with the hope that humankind "turn away from sins and to turn to God's commandments."[12] From then on, humankind would work "all the days of your life" and "by the sweat of your brow you will eat your food until you return to the ground" (Genesis 3:19).

This means that humankind will put effort into work and definitely face challenges. In the garden, food was available for the taking, but now Adam and Eve realized that the new land introduced by God would be different. Even though the ground was under a curse because of the sin committed, God gave instructions on how to operate and work the ground to produce the desired results, obtaining sustainability until death.

After God gave those instructions, man and woman had the choice to follow them. God gave us the power to choose, so we have the power to choose to work. We have the power to choose to be lazy or diligent. Hebrews 13:8 states, "Jesus Christ is the same yesterday, today, and forever." Today, these instructions are still valid, and it is a sin not to follow them.

---

[11] Thomas C. Oden, *Ancient Christian Commentary on Scripture Old Testament I* (Chicago: Fitzroy Dearborn Publishers, 2001), 15.
[12] Ibid.

Chapter 3

God's Power of Multiplication

> For the word of God is living and powerful, and sharper than any two-edged sword, piercing even to the division of soul and spirit, and of joints and marrow, and is a discerner of the thoughts and intents of the heart.
>
> —Hebrews 4:12

We serve the only one and true omnipotent God! This omnipotent God is almighty and has infinite power. The God we serve has very great and unlimited power. This same God has given us power under His authority. The one who made us has given us power. Isaiah 44:24 states, "Thus says the Lord, your Redeemer, and He who formed you from the womb: 'I am the Lord, who makes all things, who stretches out the heavens all alone, who spreads abroad the earth by myself.'"

I am the Lord who has given us the power to do the same and create a life where we can multiply or produce. His divine purpose for us is to see us utilize this power in a way to be a blessing. Even after the fall of man, we can see that Adam and Eve worked, as they instructed their sons by example to work. We find this in Genesis 4:2, "Abel kept flocks and Cain worked the soil."

Following God's instructions, sure enough, men and women

were able to work the land and survive for generations. Even though men and women succeeded in surviving by working the land and multiplying physically, spiritually, they were not. This is a key factor here. God wants His people in connection with Him not only physically but also, most importantly, spiritually. John 4:24 says, "God is Spirit, and those who worship Him must worship in spirit and truth."

When Adam and Eve were in the garden, they had communion with God. Through communion, Adam and Eve interchanged their ideas to God and vice versa. Now when they were taken out of the garden to this new place, they realized that the land was different, and in this new territory, they received different instructions.

Adam and Eve quickly realized how different and hard life was in the new place. They did not realize that just because they were in a different place with different instructions, it did not mean that God was different. God was still the same! Yes, things are different, but God is not different. I truly believe as the generations come and go, they let the devil take advantage of this in their hearts, not connecting with God spiritually, which leads them further astray from God.

God bestowed power on humankind to follow instructions under His authority to be fruitful and increase in number. God blessed them with the power to do this, but humanity took it for granted. God's heart was in pain because the human's heart was full of wickedness. Did your heart ever experience pain? My heart did. One time as I was praying, crying to God, I remembered this story.

God was hopeful that humanity could stay on track, but it did not happen, and God saw Adam and Eve fall. Roden states, "First, the multiplication of sin abbreviated that generation's time on earth (Genesis 6:1–3)."[13] This came about "that the sons of God, who were from the lineage of Seth, began to intermarry with the daughters of man, who were from the lineage of Cain."[14] Another theory when referring to the sons of God in Genesis 6:1 is that angels rebelled against God, seeing that daughters of men were beautiful and took wives for themselves. The results were the evidence of the multiplication of sin, and giants appeared (Genesis 6:4).

Even Peter mentions the disobedience of that generation who turned against God, and only Noah and his family were saved (1 Peter 3:20). Paul reminds the Corinthians this truth, "Do not be unequally yoked together with unbelievers. For what fellowship has righteousness with lawlessness" (2 Corinthians 6:14). Moreover, what communion has light with darkness?

This truth still applies to Christians today. Somewhere I read that you do not choose where to be born, where you are going to die, or who your parents or children are, but you are capable of choosing your wife or husband. So choose wisely.

Sadly, humankind forgot about God. How easily for humanity to forget God! While God never forgets about us, He is always attentive to humanity and our needs. Genesis 6:1 says, "Men began to increase in number on the earth." Physically humankind was increasing, but spiritually they were not. God did not have any problem with humankind increasing in the earth, but rather how they let evil govern their hearts. Genesis 6:5 says, "The Lord saw how great man's wickedness on the earth had become, and that every inclination of the thoughts of his heart was only evil all the time."

The Lord was grieved that he had made humankind on the earth, and his heart filled up with pain. Therefore, the Lord said,

[13] Chet Roden, *30 Days to Genesis A Devotional Commentary* (Timmonsville, S. C.: Seed Publishing Group, 2016), 25.
[14] Ibid.

"I will destroy man whom I have created from the face of the earth, both man and beast, creeping thing and birds of the air, for I am sorry that I have made them" (Genesis 6:7). God considered this choice and went forward with it is because He knew if He did not intervene, the end of it all was that humankind would let evil reign instead of seeking God.

Genesis 6:11–12 says, "The earth also was corrupt before God, and the earth was filled with violence. So God looked upon the earth, and indeed it was corrupt; for all flesh had corrupted their way on the earth." Because of humankind's hearts full of wickedness, the people living in those days were experiencing violence of all kinds. There was no respect for anyone, and people did whatever pleased them, like if there were no God in the heavens. Instead of humankind practicing the goodness of God, they practiced wickedness. Roden says, "Second, the multiplication of sin activated God's sorrow."[15] Genesis 6:5 reads, "Then the Lord saw that the wickedness of man was great in the earth, and that every intent of the thoughts of his heart was only evil continually." Then God became remorseful, creating humankind because of the multiplication of wickedness here on earth. Again, the Scripture says, "God is not a man, that he should lie, nor a son of man, that he should repent" (Numbers 23:19).

In agreement with Roden, "While God is transcendent and above human emotions as we know them, the author of Genesis was limited to the use of human language. So he tried to describe God's feelings using human words."[16] This is why we see in Genesis 6:6, the word *regretted*.

God knew if He did not intervene, humankind would have continued on this path of wickedness, and no one would see salvation. Ten generations have passed since Noah had appeared

---

[15] Roden, 26.
[16] Ibid.

and sin had multiplied greatly. Genesis 6:8 says, "But Noah found grace in the eyes of the Lord."

One person was still doing something right with the blessing bestowed on all humankind. It only took one individual to touch God's heart and find grace. It only takes one man or woman to believe and know that the same blessing found in Genesis 1:28 is still active today. It only takes one man, woman, or family for God to use to bring changes.

Sirach 44:17 says, "Noah was found perfect, righteous; in the time of wrath he became a substitute; therefore, a remnant came to be on the earth; therefore, the flood came to be." Noah means rest and comfort. God was comforted through Noah. Genesis 6:9 says, "Noah was a just man, perfect in his generations. Noah walked faithfully with God." The New International Version states, "Noah was a righteous man, blameless among the people of his time, and he walked with God"[17] (Genesis 6:9). God decided again to bestow the blessings upon him, his family, and the generations after him.

After the flood, Noah built an altar to God, and God made a covenant with Noah. Genesis 9:1 says, "So God blessed Noah and his sons, and said to them: 'Be fruitful and multiply, and fill the earth.'" Just like sin passes down the line through generations, so God's blessings and promises can pass down through a line of generations. The main reason is that God keeps His promises. Again, God here is demonstrating that He is the same God as the one in the garden and the same God who commanded Adam and Eve to be fruitful and to multiply. We find this truth in Numbers 23:19, "God is not a man, that He should lie, nor a son of man, that He should repent. Has He said, and will He not do? Or has He spoken, and will He not make it good." God does not change

---

[17] *Holy Bible: New International Version Bible (NIV)* (Grand Rapids, Mich.: Zondervan Publishing House), 1984. As found in the BibleGateway website.

His mind as humankind does. God is the opposite. He is firm with thought, and when God establishes something, He proceeds without a doubt in his mind.

God reminds Noah in Genesis 9:7, "And as for you, be fruitful and multiply; bring forth abundantly in the earth and multiply in it." God gave a sign that this covenant took place, and still today, we are able to see the rainbow. Genesis 9:14 reads, "It shall be, when I bring a cloud over the earth, that the rainbow shall be seen in the cloud."

A covenant took place between God and Noah. God sets the conditions, but humankind listens to the conditions. God allows humankind to have the power to choose to accept the conditions. One of the requirements is obedience; the second is loyalty. The same requirements were given to Adam and Eve. Many will say, "But that blessing was only for Noah and his family." In addition, many will say the main purpose of that blessing was for the physical and natural realm and not spiritually.

I am here to tell you that promise is still active today in the spiritual realm, and we can see it in the physical realm. I am here to say the blessings are for not only Adam, Noah, and their families but for all future generations. This blessing is not only for the physical or natural realm, but also it can pertain to every area of our lives. Before God declared this blessing upon Noah, God gave Noah instructions, and God put him to work. Noah worked for many years to construct an ark. Back in those days, men and women lived long days.

Noah succeeded in building the ark because he obeyed God. The blessings run toward the obedient ones. Since the beginning, God put Adam to work in the garden and to care for all the creatures. Adam succeeded until the fall. God has called many people to work, and through their work, God has blessed them more.

There is so many benefits for Christians to put practice to work. The first benefit is because God said it. It is God's plan and will for us to work. God commanded humankind to work. Again, we find this truth in Genesis 3:17–19. Second, God loves obedience. The great secret that obedience carries is opening the door for success. The devil has fooled many people into going against God's will. Obedience to God brings blessings. Every time we obey God, there are pure blessings and promises from Him. Let us read Deuteronomy 28:1–14,

> Now it shall come to pass, if you diligently obey the voice of the Lord your God, to observe carefully all His commandments which I command you today, that the Lord your God will set you high above all nations of the earth. In addition, all these blessings shall come upon you and overtake you, because you obey the voice of the Lord your God: Blessed shall you be in the city and blessed shall you be in the country. Blessed shall be the fruit of your body, the produce of your ground and the increase of your herds, the increase of your cattle and the offspring of your flocks. Blessed shall be your basket and your kneading bowl. Blessed shall you be when you come in, and blessed shall you be when you go out. The Lord will cause your enemies who rise against you to be defeated before your face; they shall come out against you one way and flee before you seven ways. The Lord will command the blessing on you in your storehouses and in all to which you set your hand, and He will bless you in the land which the Lord your God is giving you. The Lord will establish you as a holy people to Himself, just as He has sworn to you, if you keep the commandments of the Lord your God and walk in His ways. Then all peoples of the earth shall see that you are called by the name of

the Lord, and they shall be afraid of you. And, the Lord will grant you plenty of goods, in the fruit of your body, in the increase of your livestock, and in the produce of your ground, in the land of which the Lord swore to your fathers to give you. The Lord will open to you His good treasure, the heavens, to give the rain to your land in its season, and to bless all the work of your hand. You shall lend to many nations, but you shall not borrow. And the Lord will make you the head and not the tail; you shall be above only, and not be beneath, if you heed the commandments of the Lord your God, which I command you today, and are careful to observe them. So you shall not turn aside from any of the words which I command you this day, to the right or the left, to go after other gods to serve them.

Third, you will be able to sustain yourself, your family, or even others, if possible. As we know, humans cannot live without food. It is very rewarding after a hard day of work to go home and eat a good meal. Psalm 128:2 states, "When you eat the labor of your hands, you shall be happy, and it shall be well with you." The New International Version says, "You will eat the fruit of your labor; blessings and prosperity will be yours"[18] (Psalm 128:2). It pays to work because we are able to eat the fruit of our labor, and it is not in vain.

When I visited my grandparents as a young girl, I remembered they were retired. My grandfather used to labor in the fields, and after a hard workday, he would come home and eat. My grandmother usually would have the meals ready for him. Every

---

[18] Ibid.

time he came home to eat that warm, delicious food waiting for him, his face demonstrated happiness.

Fourth, our dependency comes from God. Many are blindsided, believing their dependency is from their jobs or their boss, not realizing as Christians we should depend solely on God. When we work, we are able to see that we depend on God in many ways. God gives life, the air that sustains our breathing, the seasons, health, and the strength to work. God provides work. God gives grace and favor to work.

The reality is that without God, we have nothing. Even more, God gives us the intelligence to work. God wants us to understand that without Him, we are nothing. John 15:5 says, "I am the vine, you are the branches. He who abides in me, and I in him, bears much fruit; for **without Me you can do nothing**." God wants His people to rely on Him and in His promises. God wants his people to trust in Him and His word. Many Christians have not yet come to this understanding and are living a life of mediocre.

Fifth, you feel good about yourself when you work. Something happens in your mind and within yourself when you work. Confidence shows up when you work. You have self-worth within yourself when you complete your responsibilities at work. Even if no one appreciates you or recognizes your work, God is, who is the great rewarder. As Christians, we are meant to please and honor God. Even though your supervisor or coworkers do not appreciate your work, still do it as if for the Lord. Many times, I felt underappreciated, overworked, or rejected, but that did not stop me from working as if for the Lord. Colossians 3:23 reads, "And whatever you do, do it heartily, as to the Lord and not to men." Keep pressing on as if for the Lord because, in the long run, it is God who will reward you.

Sixth, you are an asset to the community and nation. Your skills and abilities are designed for usage. Even more, you are to bless others. As a child of the Most High God, you represent the kingdom of God here on earth. Even if it does not seem like it, your time, skills, and efforts are influencing others in a way. It is influencing your community, state, or nation. Whatever level, be local or state, you are working. You are valuable, and through your skills and abilities, you can influence someone. Through your help, a smile, a positive attitude, and the ability to go the extra mile, it can make a difference in the environment that God has placed you.

Seventh, God receives glory when His people work. God receives glory when His people are working for His kingdom or in secular jobs. As long as you are where you are supposed to be and doing what you are supposed to be doing, God delights in the work of your hands. A great powerful way that God glorifies Himself is by bringing His tenth percent. This is the most powerful power God has given us. We are so able and capable of giving God His tenth percent. By giving God the tenth percent of our labor, we are honoring Him. It is a privilege to give God our tithes. Unfortunately, it is a great revelation that many Christians lack.

Chapter 4

The Power of Tithing

> Honor the Lord with your possessions and with
> the first fruits of all your increase; So your barns
> will be filled with plenty and your vats will
> overflow with new wine.
>
> —Proverbs 3:9–10

Abel and Cain brought offerings to the Lord. In addition, Noah
brought offerings to the Lord, but it was not until Abraham that
we see the first tithe recorded. This is in Genesis 14:18–20;

> "Then Melchizedek king of Salem brought out
> bread and wine; he was the priest of God Most
> High. And he blessed him and said: "Blessed be
> Abram of God Most High, possessor of heaven
> and earth; and blessed be God Most High, who
> has delivered your enemies into your hand." And
> he gave him a tithe of all."

When Abraham gave his first tithes, he experienced another
level of spiritual understanding. How did Abraham experience
another level of spiritual understanding? The answer again is
in Genesis 14:21–24. After Abraham gave the tithes, the king

of Sodom encouraged Abraham to take goods for himself, but Abraham refused. The devil knows that when you tithe, God is going to bless you.

Abraham refused and said, "I have raised my hand to the Lord, God Most High, the Possessor of heaven and earth, that I will take nothing, from a thread to a sandal strap, and that I will not take anything that is yours, lest you should say, I have made Abram rich" (Genesis 14:22–23).

Abraham told the king that if anyone made him rich, it would be God. Who is this God? The one that he just gives his tithe by faith. Abraham told the king of Sodom that he had raised his hand to God because Abraham had practiced praying to God. He practiced lifting his hands to God, a symbol of humility, adoration, or worship to God. Abraham did not give his tithes so God would make him rich; he did it for who God was in his life, the Most High God, the possessor of heaven and earth. Abraham was telling king of Sodom, "If I need anything, I just ask God, and He will provide."

Not realizing this, Abraham set himself up to meet Jehovah-Jireh when he was about to sacrifice his son Isaac (Genesis 22:14). Abraham proposed in his heart not to take anything from this king to avoid having this king say that he made Abraham rich.

Do you want to experience another level of spiritual understanding? Give your tithes; this will open your spiritual eyes to a new level of understanding. Many Christians cannot comprehend this spiritual understanding because of a lack of faith.

There are different opinions about who this King Melchizedek was. Many scholars agree that Melchizedek was a descendant of Noah, Shem. Other Christian scholars believe it was Jesus Himself. "The name Malki-Tzedek literally means 'my king' and tzedek means 'just, righteous.'" Grypeou and Spurling state, "A variety of rabbinic interpretations make it clear that Abraham is the one who gave the tithe to Melchizedek, and the emphasis is on the virtue of Abraham for his action, rather than the status of Melchizedek."[19]

This action of faith on behalf of Abraham leads him to his blessings. We see this in Genesis 24:1, "Now Abraham was old, well advanced in age; and the Lord had blessed Abraham in all things." Many want the blessings but not participate in the faithful practice of tithing. This interaction was very symbolic in many ways. In agreement with Grypeou and Spurling, "The emphasis on Abraham giving a tithe establishes the practice with him and portrays him as one who followed God's law, even if this was yet to be established."[20] A transaction took place between Melchizedek and Abraham.

Hebrews 7 speaks a lot about this transaction between Melchizedek and Abraham. Hebrew 7:2, 4 reads, "To whom also Abraham gave a tenth part of all, first being translated 'king of righteousness,' and then also king of Salem, meaning 'king of peace.' Now consider how great this man was, to whom even the patriarch Abraham gave a tenth of the spoils."

A man without genealogy, as if the Son of God, Abraham, gives his tithes by faith. Faith plays a big role because faith moves mountains. Jesus reminded His disciples about the power of having faith. Matthew 17:20 says, "So Jesus said to them, 'Because of your unbelief; for assuredly, I say to you, if you have faith as a mustard seed, you will say to this mountain, 'Move from here to there,' and it will move; and nothing will be impossible for you.'" The disciples wanted the same power as Jesus but without faith.

In the spiritual world, it does not work like that. There are principles to follow. Abraham was a man of faith. Jesus wanted His disciples to have a mindset of pure faith. Jesus wants Christians

[19] Grypeou and Spurling, *The Book of Genesis in Late Antiquity: Encounters between Jewish and Christian Exegesis* (London and Boston: Brill, 2013), 208.
[20] Ibid., 209.

to think in faith, walk in faith, see things in faith, hear things in faith, speak things in faith, and manifest things in faith.

Tithing is walking in faith. Tithing is obedience to the word of God. In obedience, there are blessings, so tithing brings blessings. Christians do not tithe because of the benefits but because we want to honor God through tithing. Let us look at Malachi 3:7–12;

> "Yet from the days of your fathers, you have gone away from my ordinances and have not kept them. Return to me, and I will return to you, says the Lord of hosts. But you said, In what way shall we return? Will a man rob God? Yet you have robbed me! But you say, "In what way have we robbed You? 'In tithes and offerings. You are cursed with a curse, for you have robbed me, even this whole nation. Bring all the tithes into the storehouse, that there may be food in My house, and try Me now in this, says the Lord of hosts, If I will not open for you the windows of heaven and pour out for you such blessing that there will not be room enough to receive it. And I will rebuke the devourer for your sakes, so that he will not destroy the fruit of your ground, nor shall the vine fail to bear fruit for you in the field, says the Lord of hosts, and all nations will call you blessed, for you will be a delightful land, says the Lord of hosts."

These verses clearly show the power of tithing and not tithing. God was rebuking the people for not tithing; now God challenges the people to bring their tithes and offerings because God will rebuke the devourer for them. When you tithe, it is not only having faith but also trusting God that He will rebuke the devourer.

Why does God give them the promise that He will rebuke the devourer? First, because God has the power to rebuke the devourer in our lives. This means that God will restrain the devil from destroying our marriages, families, churches, finances, health, and so on. In agreement with Petterson, "The idea of rebuke seems to be to restrain something so that it does not have its usual effect."[21]

Second, to challenge them to do the will of God but also because God knew that the devourer, the devil, was devouring their freedom, life, goods, families, and nation. Malachi, a minor prophet in the Old Testament, came into the picture when Judah was facing the consequences of sins. The people of Judah felt like God had abandoned them and were not loved by God. The reality is that the people of Judah were feeling like this because they were the ones who turned their backs to God. Through Malachi, God reminded the people of Judah that they were loved (Malachi 1:2). Even the priests were not honoring God. Their offerings were animals that were blind, lame, and sick (Malachi 1:8). There was no longer respect for the things of God, and the devourer brought corruption to all levels of Judah.

Tithing is not only a way of obeying God, but it is an act of worship to God. According to Taylor and Clendenen, "The issue in Malachi 3:7–12 is not tithing but apostasy. Judah is charged here with abandoning bless."[22] Even more, Taylor and Clendenen state, "By he had given retaining for themselves the tithes and other offerings they owed to God, the people showed their idolatrous hearts in placing themselves before God, and they showed their callous hearts in leaving the Levites and landless poor to fend for themselves."[23]

In his times, Nehemiah faced a challenge with the priests, Eliashib and Tobiah. The story is in Nehemiah 13:4–13. Priest

---

[21] Anthony R. Petterson, *Haggai, Zechariah & Malachi Apollos Old Testament Commentary* (Downers Grove, Ill.: IVP Academic, 2015), 338.
[22] Richard A. Taylor, and E. Ray Clendenen, *The New American Commentary Haggai, Malachi Vol 21A* (Nashville: B & H Publishing Group, 2004), 346.
[23] Ibid.

Eliashib gave Tobiah the large room that contained the offerings, tithes, and other articles that were for the Levites, singers, gatekeepers, and priests. Even more, the Levites never received their portion, and the singers went back to their regular jobs. Someone was stealing the tithes, even the offerings, and Nehemiah stated, "Why is the house of God forsaken" (Nehemiah 13:11).

Nehemiah clearly knew the truth: the stubbornness in the hearts of those men and women by not following the commandments of God would lead the nation back to the enemy's territory. In agreement with Petterson, "The neglect of the tithe clearly had wider social and religious implications. Not only would it contribute to the neglect of the temple, but it also demonstrated a failure to reflect the character of Yahweh as one who is concerned for the weak and vulnerable in society."[24] Many will say these verses only applies to the old covenant and not the new. Faith played a big role in the old covenant and the New Testament and is still playing the biggest role in Christianity.

The Pharisees and Herodian confronted Jesus by asking Him questions. "Is it lawful to pay taxes to Caesar" (Matthew 22:17)? Jesus knew their evil hearts, but the infinite wisdom of God answered, "Render therefore to Caesar the things that are Caesar's, and to God the things that are God's" (Matthew 22:21).

Jesus acknowledges and endorses that Christians must give to God the things that are of God. This includes the tithes and offerings. The ministry of Jesus was a ministry of faith, and faith is necessary for the new covenant. Tithing is an act of faith, a way to worship God, honor Him, and expand the kingdom of God. Not that God needs the money because He is the owner of gold and silver.

We find this truth in Haggai 2:8. "'The silver is Mine, and the gold is Mine,' says the Lord of hosts." When the prophet Haggai spoke these words, he referred them to the people who were

---

[24] Petterson, 107.

in Jerusalem rebuilding the temple. In agreement with Taylor and Clendenen, "Haggai argues that the economic and financial difficulties the people were experiencing—far from being an adequate excuse for their lack of substantive progress in the work that was set before them—were in reality a divine judgment directed against them because of their failures in this regard."[25]

Haggai reminded the people that placing your focus on your financial difficulties or needs before God will bring about a cycle, finding yourself in the same position. Through his words, Haggai wanted the people in Jerusalem to stir up inside, fire up, focus on God, and trust God even in regard to their needs. Because when one focuses on God, God will focus on your needs and provide them.

Now I look back on my personal experiences. One time the enemy had me in a cycle where I found an excuse for not tithing. When I was in my twenties, trying to live independently and responsibly, my paycheck was not rendering for all my needs. As a great example, I would calculate my entire bills, and the paycheck did not cover all of them. That left me without paying the tithes because I did not have enough. The cycle left me always broke and barely making it. This is exactly how many Christians are currently living. The enemy has them in this trap of barely making it unable to meet their needs. The enemy is a liar. His only job is to steal, kill, and destroy.

It was not until I decided to tithe first. As I put into practice the act of putting God first in the way I managed my finances, I soon realized that the Word of God did not go void in my life. Rather, the Word of God was active and alive, and I was able to comprehend the meaning of the verses found in Malachi 3:7–12. Render God first in all your finances and see God rebuke the enemy on your behalf. When Christians tithe, they are winning one of the greatest spiritual battles.

---

[25] Taylor and Clendenen, 97.

Again, Malachi 3:11 says, "And I will rebuke the devourer for your sakes." In agreement with Petterson, "For instance in Nahum 1:4 when the sea is rebuked, it dries up. When Satan is rebuked in Zechariah 3:2, his accusation is held back. In Malachi 3:11, when the devourer is rebuked, he is restrained."[26]

You do not have to restrain him; God will restrain the devourer for you, and this is a promise. I encourage using the power of tithing, letting God rebuke the devourer out of your life, and seeing God's promise to fulfill your life.

---

[26] Petterson, 339.

Chapter 5

The Power of Multiplication

> But the children of Israel were fruitful and
> increased abundantly, multiplied and grew
> exceedingly mighty; and the land was filled with
> them.
>
> —Exodus 1:7

The word Rabah (רָבָה), which means multiply, appears in the
Bible 226 times. Other meanings attached to this word are to
make great, enlarge, do much in respect, and exceedingly. These
are powerful words with a lot of glory. God crowned Adam and
Eve with these words, "Multiply and be fruitful." God crowned
Noah with the same words. God crowned Abraham and Jacob
until a nation came into existence.

God demonstrated His power of multiplication in many
ways. Let us look at Exodus 1:7, "But the children of Israel
were fruitful and increased abundantly, multiplied and grew
exceedingly mighty; and the land was filled with them." Again,
we see the words *multiplied* and *grew exceedingly* hand in hand.
God's promises were active and alive because the Hebrew people
were at the will of God in the right place at the right time.

How do we know they were in the right place and at the right
time? Let us take a look at what God told Abraham in Genesis

15:13–14, "Know certainly that your descendants will be strangers in a land that is not theirs, and will serve them, and they will afflict them four hundred years. In addition, the nation whom they serve I will judge; afterward they shall come out with great possessions."

Even when Pharaoh demanded the midwives kill all baby boys, God intervened. The midwives feared God, and the Word of God says that the people multiplied and grew very mighty. God created multiplication. God has the formula of how multiplication works. In math, the symbol for multiplication is *x*. It is also referred to as *product*, *times*, or *by*. Humans think they invented multiplication, but the real creator of multiplication is God.

Pharaoh resisted God, and God knew this would happen. This is why God told Moses, "So I will stretch out my hand and strike Egypt with all my wonders which I will do in its midst; and after that he will let you go" (Exodus 3:20). Multiplication is part of God's wonders. God used the power of multiplication to demonstrate His mighty power to all of Egypt. Through the power of multiplication, God crushed the enemy of the Hebrews with plagues. Not just one plague but with nine. All the fishes died in Egypt due to the waters contaminated with blood. Another plague was the countless number of frogs that appeared all over Egypt. Another plague was the locusts that ate all the crops in Egypt. The point I am trying to make here is that God will use his power of multiplication to glorify His mighty name and accomplish His divine purpose.

Through the power of multiplication, God can crush our enemies, those who have caused you pain, rejected you, belittled you, or not paid your rightly wages. Your enemies will not prosper before you but surely stand firm in the Word of God. Believe and declare Deuteronomy 28:7, "The Lord will cause your enemies who rise against you to be defeated before your face; they shall come out against you one way and flee before you seven ways."

Remember what it says in Matthew 24:35, "Heaven and earth will pass away, but my words will by no means pass away."

Again, by no means pass away, so keep believing, declaring, and trusting God because Isaiah 41:12 says, "You shall seek them and not find them—those who contended with you. Those who war against you shall be as nothing, as a nonexistent thing." God utilizes the power of multiplication not only to crush the enemy of the Hebrews but also to give them the exit out of Egypt, out of bondage, and to enter the desert to worship God.

While in the desert, God demonstrated His power of multiplication. God provided manna for the multitudes. God spoke to Moses, "Behold, I will rain bread from heaven for you" (Exodus 16:4).

Another great example of the power of multiplication is in 2 Kings 4:42–44 through the prophet Elisha. In those days, there was a famine in the land; the prophet Elisha was active in his ministry. A man "brought the man of God bread of the first fruits, twenty loaves of barley bread, and newly ripened grain in his knapsack." Elisha told the man to give it to the one hundred men before them. One can imagine the man's perplexed face. It is impossible to feed one hundred men when this food is probably for twenty people.

Elisha said again, "Give it to the people, that they may eat; for thus says the Lord: 'They shall eat and have some left over'" (2 Kings 4:43). So the man did as Elisha told him to, and behold, they ate and had some leftover.. God provides through the power of multiplication.

The Son of God, Jesus, demonstrated the power of multiplication. Through supernatural miracles and wonders, Jesus utilizes the power of multiplication to reach out to the lost. In Matthew 18:11, Jesus says, "For the Son of Man has come to save that which was lost." Jesus understood how the power of multiplication operated, and He used it in His ministry. This attracted crowds or multitudes to come and see Him. Jesus had the power to minister to the multitudes because He knew how the power of multiplication operates. Jesus had something that He was able and capable of giving, and one of them is the power of multiplication. Mark 6:34 says, "And Jesus, when he came out, saw a great multitude and was moved with compassion for them, because they were like sheep not having a shepherd. So He began to teach them many things."

The Pharisees, Sadducees, Essenes, or the Zealots acted too holy for Jesus. They rejected Jesus, yet that did not stop Him from utilizing his exceeding power to do many miracles and wonders. Many received healings, the forgiveness of sins, or liberation from demonic possessions. Through the power of multiplication, many received Jesus because He taught salvation and demonstrated the power to the multitudes. The crowds saw the many wonders that Jesus performed, such as healing the sick, giving people their faith, and providing hope in God and for their future.

One day, Jesus had multitudes before Him, and the disciples suggested He send them away, but Jesus knew the power of multiplication. The disciples said that there were only five loaves and two fish. All gospels share this story: Matthew 14:13–21, Mark 6:30–44, Luke 9:10–17, and John 6:1–15. They all have similar accounts about how Jesus looked up to heaven, blessed it, gave thanks, and distributed among all the people gathered on that day.

Whatever area in your life you are lacking, please do not hesitate to look up to heaven where your Father God is and then bless it. Pray for your lack situation and bless it. Give thanks beforehand, and break it as Jesus did. Do it in the spirit realm.

After Jesus blessed the bread and gave thanks, He broke the bread, as if saying, "It is done." The aftermath of this miracle was that every person there got satisfied. Even more, the leftovers were twelve full baskets.

God has crowned men and women to multiply. The ability is there. Men and women are capable of multiplying. We are able to multiply the works of our hands. Our labor can be exceeding. Multiplication appears in different forms, not only in the physical realm but also first in the spiritual realm. We live in a spiritual world. Then things manifest themselves in the physical world.

The multiplication of sin is active and alive. While there are still men and women living without God and practicing evil, the multiplication of sin is evident. Stevenson and et al., in regards to Ezequiel 16:25, state, "Abominations lead to multiplication of sin."[27] The multiplication of sin in the old cities of Sodom and Gomorrah led them to their own destruction.

Genesis 18:20–21 reads, "And the Lord said, 'Because the outcry against Sodom and Gomorrah is great, and because their sin is very grave, I will go down now and see whether they have done altogether according to the outcry against it that has come to Me; and if not, I will know.'"

The outcry of the consequences of sin reached to God's throne. The multiplication of sin led Israel to fall many times before her enemies, even to the point of captivity. The multiplication of sin has made nations disappear from the earth and has cursed lands, nations, and even genealogies.

A couple of years ago, I read an article online, and I was very impressed, so I even shared it with my followers over social media. It is the bloodline of Pastor John Edwards and Max Jukes. According to Winship, "The Jukes is a name given to a large family of degenerates, it is not the real name of any family, but a general term applied to forty-two different names borne by those in whose veins flows the blood of one man."[28]

The word *Jukes* has several meanings, but the interesting meaning refers to "people who are too indolent, lazy to stand up

---

[27] Kenneth Stevenson, Michael Glerup, Thomas C. Oden, and C. Thomas McCollough, *Ancient Christian Commentary on Scripture Old Testament XII Ezekiel, Daniel* (Downers Grove, Ill.: IVP Academic, 2008), 116.

[28] A. E. Winship, *Jukes-Edwards A Study in Education and Heredity* (Harrisburg, Penn.: R. L. Myers & Co., 2005), 5.

or sit up, but sprawl out anywhere."[29] Here is a brief summary of the bloodline of Jukes and Edwards:

Jukes

"Three hundred ten out of the one thousand two hundred descendants were very poor, beggars, or mendicants. (This is in a span of 2,300 years.) Three hundred died in infancy from lack of good care and good conditions. Fifty women believed to be in prostitution. Four hundred men and women destroyed early by their own wickedness. There were seven murderers. Sixty were thieves. One hundred thirty criminals."[30]

Edwards

"One hundred lawyers. Thirty judges. Thirteen college presidents, and hundred and more professors. Sixty physicians. One hundred clergymen, missionaries, and theological professors. Eighty elected to public office, including three mayors, three governors, and several members of congress, three senators, and one vice president. Sixty have attained prominence in authorship or editorial life, with 135 books of merit. Seventy-five army or navy officers."[31]

Sin is not beneficial. We all have sins. Romans 5:12 reads, "Therefore, just as through one man sin entered the world, and death through sin, and thus death spread to all men, because all sinned." Paul stated in Romans 6:1, "What shall we say then? Shall we continue in sin that grace may abound?"

Here is the answer to what he started in Romans 5:20–21, "Moreover the law entered that the offense might abound. But where sin abounded, grace abounded much more, so that as sin

---

[29] Ibid.
[30] Ibid., 8
[31] Ibid, 39.

reigned in death, even so grace might reign through righteousness to eternal life through Jesus Christ our Lord."

Schreiner states, "If the multiplication of sin sets in sharp relief the matchless character of God's grace, then sin would ultimately seem to be beneficial. In Romans 6:2–14 Paul fiercely rejects such a conclusion by arguing that the grace that believers received is so powerful that it breaks the dominion of sin."[32]

Grace comes from God, who gives it freely for all who accept Him. Even more, Schreiner states, "Grace does not simply involve forgiveness of sins; it also involves a transfer of lordship, so that believers are no longer under the tyranny of sin. As believers experience victory over sin, their confidence in a full and complete triumph over both sin and death increases."[33]

As Christians, we cannot change the past, the past mistakes of our ancestors, and our mistakes, but for sure, there is hope for the present and future. Through Jesus, we can impart a legacy to our generation and future generations. Only God can help us impart the power of multiplication for the good and break every curse so our future generations can make an impact on the world.

---

[32] Thomas R. Schreiner, *Romans Baker Exegetical Commentary of the New Testament* (Grand Rapids, Mich.: Baker Academic, 1998), 14n.
[33] Ibid.

Chapter 6

Be Fruitful

Blessed is the man who trusts in the Lord, and whose hope is the Lord. For he shall be like a tree planted by the waters, which spreads out its roots by the river, And will not fear when heat comes; but its leaf will be green, And will not be anxious in the year of drought, nor will cease from yielding fruit.

—Jeremiah 17:7–8

Jeremiah is another great prophet in the Old Testament. Jeremiah prophesied to the Southern Kingdom of Judah. Known as the weeping prophet, Jeremiah warned the people of their sins and its consequences, but the people did not listen to him. In accord with Longman, "In light of the military danger facing Judah, those who took this lesson to heart would turn to God for protection and not to their own weapons and defenses nor to political alliances with nations like Egypt."[34] The New King James Version says "yielding fruit" while other versions use "to bear fruit." Before bearing any fruit, one has to sow. Trusting in God is the first step in sowing.

---

[34] Tremper Longman III, *Jeremiah, Lamentations Understanding the Bible Commentary Series* (Grand Rapids, Mich.: Baker Books, 2008), 200.

Celeste Perez

Agriculture has come a long way. As time passed, the development of agriculture improved. Archeologists believed that "the Egyptians and Mesopotamians (c.3000 BC) were the earliest people to organize agriculture on a large scale, using irrigation techniques and manure as fertilizer. Soon after, farming formed the foundations of societies in China, India, Europe, Mexico, and Peru."[35]

Even in Roman times, the practice of crop farming was evident. Here in America and Europe, big changes occurred when the industrial period came. Even though agriculture has come a long way, the same basic formula still is vital, such as the sower needs to put the seed in fertile ground and then wait until the plant grows to see the fruits of the labor. This process can take months or even years. Two important key elements are that the sower must sow in fertile or good ground; next, the sower must have patience. To be fruitful, one must have patience.

A summer job was available to students who wanted to work in the summer. My cousins, Mari, Ben, and Moses; my sister, Jan; my brother, Papo; and I decided to try it. I do not know if you have traveled through the state of Indiana on summer days. You can see thousands of acres full of fruitful cornfields. Our job was simple, to pick up corn. The job looked simple, and it was easy money.

On the first day, we realized how hard this job was. I could hear my cousins and my brother complaining and saying that they would not come back the following day. I tried to stay focused on the job. What made it impossible to work were the bugs, humidity, sun, and complainers.

On that first day, all my cousins and my brother quit. My sister and I decided to push on until we got our first check. Sure enough, we stuck to the plan, but on that day, when we received our first check, we both got sick from heat exhaustion.

---

[35] Steve Luck, *American Desk Encyclopedia* (New York: Oxford University Press, Inc., 1998), 13.

My father and the rest of the family were happy because my sister and I were paid. Even more, out of this paycheck that night, they ate pizza on our behalf while Jan and I were sick in the bed. Yet Jan and I realized that it pays off to work, so we finished the summer strong, working in the cornfields.

That summer, I promised myself that I would never work in another cornfield. I bless those people who enjoy working in agriculture or farming, but it is not for me. I learned a lot from that summer job, and it was the first time I saw someone eat a tomato sandwich. I never knew that you could make a sandwich of pure tomato, mayonnaise, lettuce, and cheese.

The antonym of fruitful is barren, futile, disadvantageous, unfavorable, unhelpful, unprofitable, useless, worthless, impotent, sterile, unfruitful, or unproductive. Cole mentions that, "apart from calming storms (here and 6:51), Mark records Jesus as multiplying loaves (6:41 and 8:6) and withering a fig tree (11:20): he therefore accepts completely the power of Jesus over the natural world, as Son of God."[36]

Matthew and Luke recount the story of the fig tree, but only Mark tells the story in chronological order. In Mark 11:19–25, the story begins that in the morning, Jesus and His disciples were passing by a fig tree. Matthew 21:18–19 says that Jesus was hungry, seeing a fig tree on the road. Naturally, Jesus was hoping to see fruits. Unfortunately, Jesus found nothing, only leaves. The fig tree appeared to be ready and fruitful, but it was not. Matthew says in 21:19 that Jesus cursed the fig tree, and Jesus said, "Let no fruit grow on you ever again. Immediately the fig tree withered away." Jesus told His disciples in regards to knowing the season, "Now learn this parable from the fig tree: When its branch has already become tender and puts forth leaves, you know that summer is near" (Matthew 24:32).

---

[36] R. Alan Cole, *Mark Tyndale New Testament Commentaries Volume 2* (Downers Grove, Ill.: IVP Academic, 1989), 157.

There are so many lessons to learn from the fig tree. Genesis 3:7 says that Adam and Eve sewed the fig leaves together to cover themselves after they realized they were naked. Nobody told Adam and Eve to hide from God's presence, but because they sinned automatically, it led them to do things out of the character of God.

Sin brings shame and dishonor. In the calling of Nathan to become a disciple, Jesus revealed to Nathan that he was under a fig tree. When Jesus saw Nathan walking toward him, Jesus said, "Behold an Israelite indeed, in whom is no deceit" (John 1:47). Jesus knew that Nathan would accept the calling, be a disciple, and bear fruits for God's kingdom. If he were not fruitful, Jesus would have never called Nathan to be one of His disciples.

Now Jesus cursed the fig tree, and the curse brought changes to the plant. It withered, that is, dried up or wasted away. In agreement with Dockrey, Godwin, and Godwin, "Jesus placed a curse on a fig a tree that took up space and nourishment but bore no fruit."[37] Luke mentions a similar story where Jesus gave a parable in regards to a barren fig tree (Luke 13:6–9). A man planted a fig tree, but for three years, the tree did not produce. So the man suggested having the fig tree cut down.

For this man, the fig tree was taking space and nourishment from the soil but not producing. The fig tree was smart enough to take space and, moreover, nourishment from the ground or land, but it was lazy to produce. The disciples did not understand many of Jesus's parables, but in reference to cursing the fig tree, this is parallel to "the cleansing of the temple are signs of divine judgement on the empty religious practices of Israel."[38] Jesus did not approve of the temple being used as a marketplace where people were concentrating more on the goods sold in the market

---

[37] Karen Dockrey, Johnnie Godwin, and Phyllis Godwin, *The Student Bible Dictionary* (Uhrichsville, Ohio: Barbour Publishing, 2000), 93.

[38] Thomas D. Lea and David Alan Black, *The New Testament Its Background and Message*, 2nd ed. (Nashville: B & H Academic, 2003), 247.

rather using the temple for what it was meant for. This is why Jesus says, "My house should be called the house of prayer" (Matthew 21:13).

Another great message that Jesus imparted to His disciples is prayer. To be fruitful, the act of praying is a need. Jesus lived an exemplary prayerful life. Christians should live a prayerful life. Especially praying for the will of God in our daily lives is necessary. Jesus always prayed for God's will in His life. In agreement with Cole, "This is a reminder to us that prayer is not simply asking God for the pleasant things which we may desire, but an earnest yearning for, and entering into, the will of God, for ourselves and others, whether it is sweet or bitter. This was the prayer of Jesus in Gethsemane (Mark 14:35–36), and such prayers will always be answered by God."[39]

In Mark 11:21, Peter noticed the withered fig tree and said, "Rabbi, look! The fig tree which you cursed has withered away." Jesus replied, "Have faith in God." Having faith in God is part of praying because praying is talking to God. In keeping with Cole, "Faith is not chosen arbitrarily as a condition of prayer: it is the basic condition of all our relationship with God (Heb. 11:6), including prayer."[40]

Faith prayer produces fruits in the Spirit. Through prayers, God manifests the heart desires of the saints. The most important faith prayer is praying for God's will for our nation, families, friends, and lives. If any Christian wants to have a fruitful life, try faith praying. It works!

Before going off to the army, my mother shared her testimony with me. A couple of years after she married, she wanted to get pregnant, but it was unsuccessful. She thought she could not bear children. An evangelist named Yiye Avila was preaching over the radio and praying for the sick people. My mother told me that the

---

[39] Cole, *Mark Tyndale New Testament Commentaries*, 261.
[40] Ibid., 262.

evangelist encouraged all the women who were unable to have children to place their hands over their radio because he was going to pray for healings and miracles.

By faith, my mother placed her hands over the radio, believing that God would open her womb to have children. I was her first child, and less than a year after I was born, she had another. Then she had another child and another. God gave my mother seven children. For the glory of God, I shared her testimony to demonstrate that prayer is powerful! Many women in the Bible were barren. Through prayers, God opened their wombs, and they became fruitful, such as Sarah, Rebekah, Rachel, Hannah, or Elizabeth.

It breaks my heart how so many Christians go to churches that are dead spiritually because of lack of prayer. The primitive churches were full of men and women who prayed and fasted. A couple of months ago, I preached about having a prayerful life and the results. One of the examples I gave was the history of the great revival in Azusa Street, where William J. Seymour devoted himself to praying and fasting. This man, according to history, prayed for hours. Is it possible? Of course, it is because I have experienced the power of praying.

A couple of weeks later, a lovely Christian woman told me that people today do not pray for hours. I had to disagree with her and let her know that there are still intercessors, men, and women of God who have a prayerful life. It breaks my heart how the enemy has fooled churches not to have prayer meetings. Pastors are not praying and are spiritually dead. As long as the enemy keeps the church sleeping spiritually or dead spiritually, there will be no extraordinary changes, supernatural experiences, or powerful testimonies. Where is the demonstration of power? If we are followers of Jesus and we are supposed to do greater things, where is the demonstration of power?

Most of us will agree it is beneficial to have fruitful jobs, relationships, or marriage. Having a fruitful business can lead to more prospects or opportunities. Pastors want to give fruitful messages on the altar and have a fruitful congregation. Leaders want to have a fruitful ministry. Most of us want to live in a fruitful nation. As an individual of a society, one should strive to be fruitful in our society. The question to ask is: are we willing to pay the price? Acts 9:36–43 relates a story of a woman named Dorcas. She passed away, and the people of her society were sad. "This woman was full of good works and charitable deeds which she did" (Acts 9:36).

At the funeral, all the widows were weeping, showing the tunics and garments that Dorcas had made while she was with them. This was a woman who meant a lot to her society; she was fruitful in her works. Dorcas made an impact on where she was planted. As Christians, we can honestly agree that we want to be fruitful in every area of our lives. Wherever God has planted you, be fruitful. Leave a mark. Be a blessing, not a curse. Use your space to work, grow, and bear fruits.

The psalmist gives a few clues on how to become fruitful. Psalm 1:1–3 says,

> Blessed is the man who walks not in the counsel of the ungodly, nor stands in the path of sinners, nor sits in the seat of the scornful; but his delight is in the law of the Lord, and in his law he meditates day and night. He shall be like a tree planted by the rivers of water that brings forth its fruit in its season, whose leaf also shall not wither; and whatever he does shall prosper.

This is a wisdom psalm, so let us take advantage of its insights. Kartje says, "Psalm 1 contains two conceptual metaphors: life is a journey and people are plants."[41] Blessed is any person who walks away from the ungodly path that only leads to destruction. In the ungodly path, there is only sin and rebellion against God. The good path leads to salvation; the bad path leads to destruction.

In this life journey, all of us make daily decisions. Many times, we need counsel. Let God be your first counsel. God is wisdom, and in Him are the answers that oftentimes we need and seek. In the past, I made the mistake of listening to ungodly people for counsel instead of seeking God for His help. Unfortunately, the decision I made brought in my life many frustrations and unsettled matters. Oftentimes, making the wrong decisions can be costly, time-consuming, and wasted years.

The psalmist encourages its readers to delight themselves in the law of the word. Even more, the psalmist says to meditate on the word *day* and *night*, for when you do this, for sure whatever you do will prosper. When you get up in the morning, give God your first thoughts. Seek Him in the morning. Take time to meditate on the Bible. Read it, memorize it, absorb it, speak it, declare it, and pray with the Word. Isaac, son of Abraham, became a prosperous man. Genesis 24:63 says, "He went out to the field one evening to meditate, and as he looked up, he saw camels approaching." Isaac practiced meditation. He purposefully took time to meditate. As Christians, we should do the same. Intentionally set time apart to meditate on the Scripture. It is a form of reverence to God.

Kartje mentions, "The righteous are well-rooted, they are near a source of life (water), they yield fruit at the proper time, and they never wither. A plant's health is measured solely by its fruitfulness: by the vitality of its foliage and the abundance of its produce."[42] This reminds me of the woman of Samaria who came

---

[41] John Kartje, *Wisdom Epistemology in the Psalter A Study of Psalms 1, 73, 90, and 107* (Berlin and Boston: De Gruyter, 2014), 81.

[42] Kartje, *Wisdom Epistemology in the Psalter*, 83.

to the well seeking water. Jesus told her, "But whosoever drinketh of the water that I shall give him shall never thirst; but the water that I shall give him shall be in him a well of water springing up into everlasting life" (John 4:14). Jesus is the living water! We need to be rooted in Him if we want to have a fruitful life. How can we be blessings to others if we are not rightly rooted in the Word or Him? How can we be a testimony to others if we are walking on the ungodly path? We must pay the sacrifice, be godly, walk on the godly path, meditate on the word, and be doers of the word.

How do you know if you are a doer of the word? By your fruits. Jesus warned His disciples to be aware of false prophets. Then Jesus utilized a parable about the fruits. I bring this passage, Matthew 7:16–20, for the purpose of bringing about more insight for the word *fruitful*. Jesus said,

> You will know them by their fruits. Do men gather grapes from thorn bushes or figs from thistles? Even so, every good tree bears good fruit, but a bad tree bears bad fruit. A good tree cannot bear bad fruit, nor can a bad tree bear good fruit. Every tree that does not bear good fruit is cut down and thrown into the fire. Therefore by their fruits, you will know them.

What fruits are you bearing? When the world sees you, do they see good or bad fruits?

Even Paul shared to the Galatians about bearing fruits. Even more, Paul made a distinction between the works of the flesh versus the fruits of the spirit. Either we are fruitful in the spirit or operating under the flesh. Galatians 5:19–23 says,

> Now the works of the flesh are evident, which are: adultery, fornication, uncleanness, lewdness, idolatry, sorcery, hatred, contentions, jealousies,

outbursts of wrath, selfish ambitions, dissensions, heresies, envy, murders, drunkenness, revelries. But the fruit of the Spirit is love, joy, peace, longsuffering, kindness, goodness, faithfulness, gentleness, self-control.

There are two fruits: the desire of the flesh and the desire of the spirit. The two live in a body, but the two do not tolerate each other. This is why Paul said in Galatians 6:8, "For he who sows to his flesh will of the flesh reap corruption, but he who sows to the Spirit will of the Spirit reap everlasting life."

You want to be fruitful and prosperous. Consider and meditate on Psalm 1. The people of Israel had many seasons where they were fruitful. If you check, the time they were fruitful was when they were following the law, but every time they forgot about God's commandments, the nation usually backslid. This repeatedly occurred in Israel. And God continually intervened and showed them the path again. In a final word for this chapter, Galatians 6:7 says, "Do not be deceived, God is not mocked; for whatever a man sows, that he will also reap."

Chapter 7

Blessed Israel

I will bless those who bless you, and I will curse
him who curses you; And in you all the families
of the earth shall be blessed.

—Genesis 12:3

God keeps His promises throughout the ages. God told Abraham,
"I will bless those that bless you, and I will curse those that curse
you." Throughout history, we have seen how God's word still
stands. Pharaoh saw that the Hebrews were mighty in Egypt,
so he decided to afflict them, but that plan did not work either.
According to Cole, in regards to Pharaoh's labor camps, "Forced
labor was an old principle in highly centralized Egypt, as in all
ancient world: neither pyramids nor Nile canals would have been
possible without it."[43] That plan did not work well so, Pharaoh's
next plan was to deliberately exterminate the Hebrews by killing
the baby boys. Pharaoh asked the midwives, Shiphrah and Puah,
to kill all baby boys.

Shiphrah and Puah did not follow Pharaoh's order; rather,
they feared God. They decided to lie to Pharaoh, and their excuse

[43] R. Alan Cole, *Exodus an Introduction and Commentary Tyndale Old Testament Commentaries*, Vol. 2 (Downers Grove, Ill.: IVP Academic, 1973), 61.

was, "Because the Hebrew women are not like the Egyptian women; for they are lively and give birth before the midwives come to them" (Exodus 1:19). The interesting thing about this story is that both women lied and protected the Hebrew baby boys. The Scripture says that God dealt well with the midwives, and He provided a household for them, meaning that He blessed the midwives. Even Phaorah's daughter eventually found Moses on the riverbank and took him in as her own, ignoring her father's requests to kill the Hebrew baby boys. For sure, we can see that the nation that goes against Israel or becomes its enemy will face tragic consequences.

In agreement with Cole, "The whole vain attempt to wipe out the people of God finds its parallel in the New Testament attempt by Herod to destroy a generation of babies at Bethlehem (Matthew 2:16). But, as in the New Testament, God's chosen agent is protected neither pharaoh nor Herod can stand in the way of God's plan."[44] God frustrates the enemy's plans. If you stay faithful to God, He will frustrate the enemy's plan against your life and that of your family.

Another great story of the Bible is Rahab. In Joshua 2, we see Joshua getting ready to take possession of Jericho and send spies there. There was already terror in the walls of Jericho because Rahab confessed to the spies that the people of Jericho had heard the mighty works of God.

Rahab provided a space for the spies to hide. She protected the spies and lied to those seeking to kill them. The Scripture says that Joshua spared Rahab, her father's household, and all she had. Space was provided for Rahab and her family to be part of the Israelites. She married Salmon and had a son named Booz, who became King David's grandfather. God included her in the genealogy of Jesus.

Israel's enemies will not prosper, but God will frustrate their

---

[44] Cole, *Exodus an Introduction and Commentary*, 64.

plans. Pharaoh commanded all his people to cast all Hebrew baby boys in the river to die. Pharaoh died as a result of drowning. Cole states, "Jewish expositors have seen parallels to pharaoh's action in the attempted genocide of Israel by Hitler and others: Christian expositors have sought such parallels in the bitter persecutions suffered by the church throughout her history."[45]

The same happened to Haman in Esther 3. He conspired to kill all the Jews. Esther 5:14 says that Haman made gallows to hang Mordecai. His plans were frustrated. Even his wife Zeresh said to him, "If Mordecai, before whom you have begun to fall, is of Jewish descent, you will not prevail against him but will surely fall before him" (Esther 6:13). The same gallows Haman prepared against Mordecai were later utilized for Haman and his ten sons. Even more, the date that Haman set to kill all the Jews was on that same day that the Jews killed and destroyed their enemies, which were seventy-five thousands of their enemies. When Hitler and his men started messing with the Jews, the fall of Germany was evident. Hitler killed many Jews, and he ended up killing himself.

Israel is a blessing to the nations. Christianity owes a lot to the nation of Israel, such as our faith, the Torah, the books in the New Testament, our Savior Jesus, and so much more. The United States has had the privilege to have Jews be part of its history. A great example is Haym Solomon. History tells us that Haym Solomon used his own money to help and bless the beginning of this great nation. Stiefel mentions,

> Indeed army supply was often the responsibility of Haym Solomon (1740–85), a major broker dealing with the U.S. government's Office of Finance. As a resident of both New York and Philadelphia and with a thriving financial business, Solomon used

---

[45] Ibid.

> his commercial connections and especially his bills
> of exchange, tendered between St. Eustatius and
> Europe, to help supply the Continental Army.[46]

This Jewish man helped finance the Continental Army, in which George Washington was the commander in chief. Even more, McCraw says, "Solomon sold bonds issued by Congress, lent money to legislators and others, and invested his own funds in the war effort."[47] Sadly, he died pennilessly.

Probably, like this man, many Jews believed that the United States would someday help Israel or its people. Many Jews came to Europe and the Americas to seek a new and better life. The United States, through President Truman, was the first country to recognize Israel as a state. Benson related to an occasion when the chief rabbi of Israel visited President Truman. According to Benson, "In early 1949 told him (President Truman), 'God put you in your mother's womb so that you could be the instrument to bring about the rebirth of Israel after two thousand years,' tears rose to the president's eyes."[48]

Even more, "The rabbi then opened the Bible that he was carrying with him and read the words of King Cyrus from the Book of Ezra: 'The Lord God of heaven hath given me all the kindness of the earth; and he hath charged me to build Him a house at Jerusalem, which is in Judah.'"[49] What an extraordinary event that was when the Jews were able to go back to their homeland.

---

[46] Barry L. Stiefel, *Jewish Sanctuary in the Atlantic World A Social and Architectural History* (Columbia, S. C.: University of South Carolina Press, 2014), 160.

[47] Thomas K. McCraw, *The Founders and Finance* (Cambridge, Mass.: The Belina P Press of Harvard University Press, 2012), 336.

[48] Michael T. Benson, *Harry S. Truman and the Founding of Israel* (Westport, Conn.: Praeger Publishers, 1997), 190.

[49] Ibid.

The Jewish are remarkable people. Years ago, I read a positive statement and truth concerning the Jewish people.

> Jews make up less than two-tenths of a percentage point of the world's population. Yes, only .02 percent-yet they represent more than 10 percent of the Forbes 400 list of the world's wealthiest people, more than 10 percent of the Fortune list of the CEOs of the 500 largest corporations in the world, and almost 30 percent of all the Nobel Prize winners.[50]

A great example of Jewish ancestry is Albert Einstein, who contributed a lot through his inventions. Pastor John Hagee wrote a book under the title, *In the Defense of Israel*. Here, Pastor Hagee gives a brief summary of the Jewish contribution to society.[51] Many people in the past, even today, question the success of the Jewish people that the Jewish people have experienced persecution for their success. According to Brackman and Jaffe, "Henry Ford self-published a book about 'the Jewish problem' which urged his fellow citizens to stand in the way of this foreign race that was becoming too successful too quickly."[52] Even more, "Adolf Hitler published a similar book, Mein Kampf."[53] Both books barely make a sound today, but the Bible, the Word of God, still stands today.

Christians around the world should be encouraged about the success of the Jewish people and learn from them. Brackman

---

[50] Rabbi Levi Brackman and Sam Jaffe, *Jewish Wisdom for Business Success Lessons from the Torah and Other Ancient Texts* (New York: American Management Association, 2008), xiii.

[51] John Hagee, *In Defense of Israel* (Lake Mary, Fla: Frontline A Strang Company, 2008), 104.

[52] Brackman and Jaffe, xiv.

[53] Ibid.

and Jaffe say, "We believe that the root cause of Jewish success in business lays in the book Jews hold most dear and sacred-the Torah."[54] The Torah is composed of the first five books of the Bible: Genesis, Exodus, Leviticus, Numbers, and Deuteronomy. Acts 3:25 says, "You are sons of the prophets, and of the covenant which God made with our fathers, saying to Abraham, 'And in your seed all the families of the earth shall be blessed.'"

Christians are adoptive sons and daughters. Paul wrote to the Galatians, reminding them of this truth. Even though the Christians in Galatia were dealing with Judaizers who were teaching legalism, Paul encouraged them to stay focused on who they are in Christ through faith. Galatians 3:16 reads, "Now to Abraham and his Seed were the promises made. He does not say, 'And to seeds,' as of many, but as of one, 'And to your Seed,' who is Christ." Galatians 3:29 reads, "And if you are Christ's, then you are Abraham's seed, and heirs according to the promise."

Christians should pray for Israel because there is an active promise. Again, Genesis 12:3 says, "I will bless those who bless you, and I will curse him who curses you; and in you, all the families of the earth shall be blessed." This promise is not only for the Old Testament but for today as well. Years ago, the news hit about Hugo Chavez, the dictator of Venezuela, who cursed Israel in 2010, and in 2013, he died of cancer. Psalm 122:6 says, "Pray for the peace of Jerusalem: May they prosper who love you." This enough should encourage any Christian to pray for Israel.

"During the Old Testament period, Jerusalem was the place where God made is special presence known to his people. It was the center of the world, and so pilgrims traveled to that city and prayed for its peace and security."[55] Jerusalem, also known as the City of David, was an important city. Still today, Jerusalem is an

---

[54] Ibid.
[55] Tremper Longman III, *Tyndale Old Testament Commentaries Psalms* (Downers Grove, Ill.: IVP Academic, 2014), 418.

important city. In King David's time, "Jerusalem is not part of the tribes of Israel, but it is the spiritual and political center of a united Israel."[56] Today, it is still so. Even more, for Christians, the city of Jerusalem is the prophetic clock with confirmation of events that have taken place, are taking place and will take place.

Many probably will say that Christians should pray for the peace of the world. Yes, Christians should pray for the peace of the world, for the peace of each nation, but according to the Scripture in Psalm 122:6, Christians should include the city of Jerusalem in their prayers. There is a need to pray for the peace of Jerusalem. Christians need to pray for the welfare of Jerusalem. Many enemies surround Israel, and Israel needs our prayers. King David finishes saying, "May they prosper who love you" (Psalm 122:6). May God prosper those that love you, oh Israel! What a powerful statement from King David. Be encouraged to pray for the nation of Israel, especially the peace of Jerusalem.

---

[56] Longman, *Tyndale Old Testament*, 417.

Chapter 8

Parents Leading by Example

But Jesus answered them, "My Father has been
working until now, and I have been working."
—John 5:17

God gave us a pattern to imitate Him, and one of them is to work.
Let's look at the first family who walked on earth. Adam and Eve gave
an example to their first sons, Cain and Abel. We see this in Genesis
4:2, where Cain worked the soil and Abel kept the flocks. Vos states,
"There is no suggestion that one of these occupations was better than
the other. Very possibly, both had already been pursued by Adam."[57]

These two sons learned from their parents that they had to
work to sustain themselves. Children learned from their parents
in regards to work. It became custom for children to learn the
trade of their parents to survive. God Himself worked six days,
and on the seventh day, He rested. In agreement with Anders and
Martin, "Man should work six days and rest on the seventh. God
knew the effects of constant physical toil not only on the body but
on man's spirit as well."[58]

---

[57] J. G. Vos, *Genesis* (Pittsburgh: Crown & Covenant Publications,
2006), 46.

[58] Glen S. Martin, *Holman Old Testament Commentary Exodus, Leviticus,
Numbers* (Nashville: Broadman and Holman Publishers, 2002), 98.

Work is God's plan for humanity. In agreement with Lennox, "Work was intended by God in the first place-experiencing his rule and righteousness. His intention is that our work becomes an integral part of the process of character development."[59] The argument about the seventh day will not be argued here since there are different opinions. The argument here is that work is part of God's purpose for humanity.

2 Kings 4:18 says, "And the child grew. Now it happened one day that he went out to his father, to the reapers." This child was a miracle baby. God used Elisha to prophesy into the Shunammite woman, and in due time, she gave birth to a healthy baby boy. The child grew, and now he went to his father. This means "the boy had grown to the age where he was able to be in the fields with his father."[60] The father was at work with the reapers, people who worked in the harvest and did the gathering of the harvest. Parents should allow their children to be around them so they can learn how to conduct themselves publicly, how to work with people, and overall learn how to work.

Maybe you might say, "But I cannot take my children to work." Probably not, but children can see their mom and dad getting up early. Maybe talk to your children about your work and what you do. This will help your children have an image of you working, and it will help them see that having a job or employment is a serious matter, part of life, and a necessity that one day they will need to follow.

Parents who have never worked expect their own children to sustain themselves and go to work. Realistically, how can these parents expect their own children to work when their own children have never seen them work or maintain a job and hardly provide the necessities for their own children? If parents never

---

[59] John C. Lennox, *Joseph: A Story of Love, Hate, Slavery, Power, and Forgiveness* (Wheaton, Ill.: Crossway, 2019), 123.

[60] Max Anders and Gary Inrig, *Holman Old Testament Commentary* (Nashville: Broadman & Holman Publishers, 2003), 223.

worked, there is a high probability that their children will never work either. Many times the children are the image of their parents unless God intervenes powerfully, which I have seen where children are apt to learn and make positive changes for themselves and their future generations.

As a daughter's pastor, at a young age, I was active in helping my dad and mom in the ministry. Not only did I go to school, but I also helped Mom in the house and Dad at church, including his work for the seminar. In fact, there are so many children exposed to work in the ministry at an early age, and you know what? God oftentimes reveals His calling to children too. At a young age, children can have amazing experiences with God. Parents should be there to support them and help them answer questions that they might have. It is beautiful to see children having trusting, open conversations with their parents.

Eli was the spiritual father of the prophet Samuel. From an early age, the Levites surrounded Samuel. In addition, Samuel had a glance at the high priest's full potential work. Numbers 3:5–10 gives a brief description of the Levite's duties. Wenham mentions,

> Levites duties were to serve Aaron the priest and to minister to God such as transporting and erecting the tabernacle. They only had to do this heavy work whenever the camp was on the move. However, they had to be permanently on guard, ready to kill any unauthorized person approaching the tent of meeting, its furniture or the altar like a policeman.[61]

---

[61] Gordon J. Wenham, *Numbers An Introduction and Commentary* (Downers Grove, Ill.: IVP Academic, 1981), 79.

At a young age, Samuel was actively working, and we see this in 1 Samuel 3:1, "Now the boy Samuel ministered to the Lord before Eli." This young boy was ministering, but under the leadership of the priest, Eli. In addition, Samuel learned the duties of the high priest. Eli, the high priest, "alone had the right to handle the sacrificial blood, touch the altar and to enter the tent of meeting. Eli was the authoritative teachers of the nation, the official mediator between God and Israel. With great privilege went immense responsibility."[62]

God called the young boy Samuel, but Eli recognized that the Lord was calling the boy. Later, this young boy became a well-known prophet in Israel. As a prophet, Samuel carried his duties to God with honor, loyalty, and dedication. Samuel is proof that children are capable of learning about duties and responsibilities at a young age, including all about work.

Another young boy who worked hard and defended his father's sheep was David. Jesse was the father of David. On one occasion, Jesse answered to the prophet Samuel, "There remains yet the youngest, and there he is, keeping the sheep" (1Samuel 16:11). As a shepherd, this young boy encountered not only harsh weather but also many sleepless nights. Later on, this young David obeyed his father and took food to his brothers, who were in a battle against the Philistines. While there, Goliath was defying the camp of Israel. Young David took courage. 1 Samuel 17:34–36 says,

> But David said to Saul, Your servant used to keep his father's sheep, and when a lion or a bear came and took a lamb out of the flock, I went out after it and struck it, and delivered the lamb from its mouth; and when it arose against me, I caught it by its beard, and struck and killed it. Your servant has killed both lion and bear; and this

---

[62] Ibid.

uncircumcised Philistine will be like one of them, seeing he has defied the armies of the living God.

David proudly related this story to King Saul. This is exactly what is supposed to happen when someone works. There is a sense of pride and confidence when responsibilities are accomplished. Young David learned to work, and he learned from his father, Jesse. It's important to see how adults, parents, and even leaders can influence their children.

When Jesus was growing up, he learned his father's trade, carpentry. Mark 6:3 refers to Jesus, "Is this not the carpenter, the Son of Mary, and brother of James, Joses, Judas, and Simon?" Clearly, Joseph taught his son, Jesus, the trade of carpentry. Jesus oftentimes saw his father attend to his clients, get up, find wood or tools, work long hours, or sweat. Joseph led by example.

Even the apostle Paul, who was a spiritual father to so many Christians, warned against idleness. 2 Thessalonians 3:6–9 reads,

> But we command you, brethren, in the name of our Lord Jesus Christ, that you withdraw from every brother who walks disorderly and not according to the tradition which he received from us. For you yourselves know how you ought to follow us, for we were not disorderly among you; nor did we eat anyone's bread free of charge, but worked with labor and toil night and day, that we might not be a burden to any of you, not because we do not have authority, but to make ourselves an example of how you should follow us.

Beale states, "What it means that some are behaving in a disorderly manner: they are working but are busybodies. They are not working in order to support themselves with food, clothing, and shelter."[63] Even more, "Not only are they passively out of order by not busying themselves with proper work, but they are actively unruly by busying themselves with wrong activities."[64]

The apostle Paul realized that they were lazy Christians professing the name of Jesus but not giving an example of Jesus. Wherever Paul went, not only did he spread the gospel to the Jews or Gentiles but also he worked. Paul was a tentmaker. When he came to the city of Corinth, there he worked as a tentmaker and preached the gospel (Acts 18:3).

Paul's tone of voice is serious about this subject, firm and determined. Paul told the church to withdraw from that person because that individual could influence others to do the same. Some theologians believe that this specific person, the one whom Paul was referring to, was not working due to eschatological beliefs, for instance, that the day of the Lord was so soon that it was not necessary to work (2 Thessalonians 2). Either way, the person needed to eat to survive, so Paul encouraged him to keep on working. Paul said, "If you do not work, do not eat as well" (2 Thessalonians 3:10).

Paul called them disorderly. Beale agrees, "The disorderly are out of place because they hinder the spread of the gospel, not only by disseminating and following the false teaching but by not following the divine order of creation in which all humans are to work in order to sustain one's existence."[65]

God is a God of order, not a God of disorderly. The world has its eyes on the Christians, on us, so living lives in order is necessary to testify about Jesus and for the sake of the gospel. Sadly, many Christian-professing followers of Jesus today are giving twisted messages to the world. Incredibly, those so-called Christians have not realized that they are trapped in a mediocrity mental state of mind, just as the devil wants them to be.

---

[63] G. K. Beale, *1–2 Thessalonians The IVP New Testament Commentary Series* (Downers Grove, Ill.: IVP Academic, 2003), 251.

[64] Ibid.

[65] Ibid., 252–253.

Chapter 9

The Calling to the Ministry

For many are called, but few are chosen.
—Matthew 22:14

Foremost, God does not call a lazy person to work in His godly kingdom. Every person on this earth has a God-given purpose, but many do not know this. Still, today God keeps calling out to His people, inviting them for a bigger purpose, but many are not ready, others do not think they are ready, some are not willing to pay the price, more are scared, and a few are just plain lazy. I have seen how God calls people to the ministry, especially people working in full-time jobs.

For many, it is a process. At first, they were scared, but trusting God made the transition much easier. Others are working both full-time in the ministry and the secular world. Some are working full-time in God's kingdom and part-time to the side. Many work full-time in a secular job but do work at night at church or in ministry. Now there are those who are working full-time with a secular job, and God has spoken to them about a full-time ministry.

Let us not forget that God hires qualified Christians for a specific job, and one of those qualifications is that they must be willing to sacrifice time to work for Him. There are many examples in the Bible of people working and God calling them to their divine purpose or for a specific reason. God Himself loves to be at work, and He does not want people in the ministry pretending to be working when in reality, they do not know the blessing of actually getting up early in the morning to go to work. Even more, God has called people to be full-time in the ministry, and God knows if they were faithful to Him in those secular jobs, they are capable of being faithful in the ministry as well.

Exodus 3:1 says, "Now Moses was tending the flock of Jethro his father-in-law, the priest of Midian. And he led the flock to the back of the desert, and came to Horeb, the mountain of God." Before God called Moses to be the leader of Israel, he was working full time for his father-in-law. Hamilton says, "Shepherding is what Moses has been doing for a good long while. If one thinks about it, it is a good preparation for another kind of shepherding to which God will call Moses."[66]

The duties of a shepherd are not easy. For instance, one has to make sure that all flocks make it back home safely. It's pretty much a job that entails a lot of supervision and guidance. Remember that Moses fled out of Egypt, leaving an ugly past, and started a new life in Midian. Moses even named his son Gershom, meaning "I have been a stranger in a foreign land" (Exodus 2:22). Yet he adapted himself to this new life, and in Exodus 3, one can tell he was a hardworking man. Probably he thought that his life would remain as just that, working in the desert attending the animals.

In reality, God had other plans for Moses. It is interesting to note, "God does not reveal himself to Moses so spectacularly when Moses is praying, or fasting, or meditating, or engaging in some profound metaphysical thought. It happens while he is alone, working, and probably unexciting menial work at that."[67]

---

[66] Victor P. Hamilton, *Exodus An Exegetical Commentary* (Grand Rapids, Mich.: Baker Academic, 2011), 45.
[67] Ibid.

Moses's job was preparing him for God's plans for his life, which was a divine calling and a divine purpose. It was a perfect day for an unexpected visit from the Almighty God, one that changed Moses's life forever.

The calling of Gideon came while working. Judges 6:11 says, "Now the Angel of the Lord came and sat under the terebinth tree which was in Ophrah, which belonged to Joash the Abiezrite, while his son Gideon threshed wheat in the winepress, in order to hide it from the Midianites." Radmacher, Allen, and House state, "The fact that Gideon was forced to thresh wheat hidden inside winepress shows again the desperate state the Israelites were in."[68]

God was aware of the hard things that the people of Israel were enduring. However, this does not limit God to seek someone in whom he could entrust the task of freeing the people of Israel from the hands of the Midianites. God encouraged Gideon in verse 14, "Then the Lord turned to him and said, 'Go in this might of yours, and you shall save Israel from the hand of the Midianites. Have I not sent you?'"

When God entrusts someone with a specific task, it is because He knows that such a person is capable of doing it. Gideon doubted the calling in his life. How many times have you doubted God? God knows you are capable of carrying your purpose here on earth. Oftentimes doubts can delay the purpose of your life. I often doubted God. I knew I had a calling and a purpose, but I wanted others to see it first, but God wanted me to see it first. Instead of relying on others to see that God was calling me, God wanted me to see it first, accept it first, and believe it, and then others would see it. Gideon said, O my Lord, how can I save Israel? Indeed my clan is the weakest in Manasseh, and I am the least in my father's house" (Judges 6:15). What Gideon did not know is that God is an expert in calling people with specific

---

[68] Earl Radmacher, Ron Allen, and H. Wayne House, *Compact Bible Commentary* (Nashville: Thomas Nelson, 2004), 148.

missions. God promised to be with him, and Gideon asked for a sign that God had given it to him.

Another great example is Ruth. Ruth faced challenges of changes, causing her to leave her country and follow Noemi. Her attitude was extraordinary. She did not complain but rather stayed positive throughout the journey and the new challenges, and this was why God chose her for a divine purpose. Out of necessity and willingness to work, Ruth begged Noemi to let her go to work. Ruth demonstrated she was a hardworking woman, as well as bold and not afraid. Ruth 2:2–3 says, "Please let me go to the field, and glean heads of grain after him in whose sight I may find favor. Then she left, and went and gleaned in the field after the reapers." Ruth saw this as an opportunity because "the Law of Moses allowed the poor to glean in the farmers' field (Leviticus 23:22)."[69] What adversities or challenges are you facing?

Like Ruth, maintain a positive outlook because no doubt God is powerful to show you the opportunities in the midst of the challenges you are facing. Be encouraged and bold like Ruth. Not only did Ruth obtain favor before God, but she did so before Boaz and the community. Ruth became part of King David's genealogy, and Matthew mentions her in 1:5–6 as part of Jesus's genealogy. Other examples are found in the following:

• 1 Kings 19:19–21. Elisha was plowing with twelve yokes of oxen, and Elisha was driving the twelfth pair of oxen. When Elijah threw his cloak around him, Elisha knew God was calling for the ministry, and after he did what he had to do, Elisha followed Elijah and became his attendant.
• Nehemiah 1–2. We can clearly see that Nehemiah was troubled by the situation in Jerusalem, so he mourned, fasted, and prayed before God. Nehemiah was before King Artaxerxes, and his job was to serve the king like a butler. Nehemiah was

---

[69] Ibid., 159.

the one who tasted the wine first before the king drank it. Nehemiah felt the calling in his heart, and he was able to go to Jerusalem and inspect the walls. Later Nehemiah became one of the main leaders in rebuilding the wall of Jerusalem. You know what? God of heavens gave him the victory!

- Matthew 4:18. The Bible says that as Jesus was walking beside the Sea of Galilee, he saw two brothers: Simon, called Peter, and his brother, Andrew. They were fishermen, and in that hour, they were working, casting a net into the lake. God made them fishers of men, and through their ministry, many received salvation.

- Matthew 4:21. He went on and saw two other brothers, James and John, the sons of Zebedee. They were in their boat with their father, Zebedee, getting their nets ready. They were fishermen. Jesus called them, and at once, they left the boat and their father and went with him.

- Mark 2:14. As he walked along, he saw Levi, son of Alphaeus, sitting at the tax collector's booth. He was a tax collector. "Follow me," Jesus told him, and Levi got up and followed him.

- Acts 9:4–6. God called Saul, later known as Paul, while he was working full time persecuting the Christians. As of matter of fact, Saul was on his way to Damascus to take Christians as prisoners and bring them back to Jerusalem, but God intervened and instructed him on what to do. Paul became a living testimony of Christ Jesus, and through his ministry, many lives were changed forever.

There are so many examples of how people received their divine calling. To work in the ministry, many times, God will test the servants. I have learned and seen how God has called many people to the ministry, and several of them had full-time jobs. This is why it is crucial for Christians, wherever you are at work, to do it as for God because maybe God is testing you in this arena. The calling of God is serious business. There must be a willingness and a humble heart to accept the divine calling because, through it, many will see the power of multiplication. Proverbs 21:25 says, "The desire of the lazy man kills him, For his hands refuse to labor." The next verse, 26, states, "He covets greedily all day long, But the righteous gives and does not spare."

Chapter 10

Increasing Glory

Into His likeness with ever-increasing glory.
—2 Corinthians 3:18

God wants to give an increasing glory and to take us from glory to glory, and God has given His people the power to go from glory to glory. In addition, God can take us from strength to strength; like Psalm 84:7 says, "They go from strength to strength." It is up to us if we want to do His will. The people of Israel had a vast past of turning their backs away from God and not following His ways. When the prophet Ezekiel emerged, he prophesied about the destruction of Jerusalem, the judgments coming to nearby nations, and the reconciliation between God and Israel. Finally, talked about the return of exiles.

Yet to this prophet, God revealed the truth. Even though Israel had fallen due to disobedience, idolatry, and many other sins, God still had a plan for Israel. Ezekiel 36:11 says, "I will multiply upon you man and beast; and they shall increase and bear young; I will make you inhabited as in former times, and do better for you than at your beginnings. Then you shall know that I am the Lord." God reminds the people of Israel that He still is a God of multiplication, increase, blessings, restoration, and renewal, even if the people of Israel failed Him. This demonstrates the mercy of God and His love for His people.

Jesus spoke many things, but he encouraged His disciples, "In the world, you will have tribulation, but be of good cheer, I have overcome the world" (John 16:33). Even though Christianity holds the truth about the way of salvation, we serve a mighty God. We are not exempt from experiencing hardships. The God of multiplication will allow us to go through experiences not only to demonstrate His power but also to take us from glory to glory.

Job experienced great hardship. One day, he lost everything: his livelihood, children, and status. His known world became an unknown world, yet Job fell to the ground and worshiped God.

Job acknowledged God in his trials. "Naked I came from my mother's womb, and naked shall I return there. The Lord gave, and the Lord has taken away; blessed be the name of the Lord" (Job 1:21). Job acknowledged that God gave him all he had, even though his wife, in her anguish, told Job to "curse God and die" (Job 2:9). Yet Job maintained his integrity toward God, saying, "Shall we indeed accept good from God, and shall we not accept adversity" (Job 2:10).

Oftentimes God will allow afflictions and hardships in our lives to demonstrate the power of multiplication to us. During the aftermath of all the afflictions and hardships, for sure, God will bring His blessings. I will add, oftentimes God does not wait until the aftermath of the trial, but even during the trial, God's goodness and mercies can be experienced. I can testify to this because while going through my cancer journey, the power of the multiplication of God's goodness became evident. God touched so many people to bless me tremendously in many different ways.

Before Job lost everything, the God in heavens acknowledged that Job was a "servant, there is none like him on the earth, a blameless, upright man, and one who fears God" (Job 1:8). While Job was enjoying the multiplication of God on earth, the devil was accusing him in heaven. The story of Job is a great example, proving how things manifest themselves first in the spiritual realm. Satan knew that Job had divine protection because Satan asked God,

> Have You not made a hedge around him, around his household, and around all that he has on every side? You have blessed the work of his hands, and his possessions have increased in the land. But now, stretch out Your hand and touch all that he has, and he will surely curse You to Your face. (Job 1:9–11)

In the spiritual realm, God made a hedge around him and the things of Job. God placed a spiritual boundary so the devil would not devour his things or touch him. It was not until God allowed the devil to touch Job's health, family and wealth that Job experienced loss. Even though his friends came to console Job, it did not go well. His friends inferred that Job was in that state of poverty and sickness because he had sinned against God. People are easy to judge, especially those who are closer to you.

Job's friends even tried to console him. They misjudged him. Surely the cause of all Job's misfortune was due to sinning against God. Bildad encouraged Job to repent from his sins. Bildad said truthful words to Job, but that truth was for Bildad to acknowledge.

Bildad said, "If you would earnestly seek God and make your supplication to the Almighty if you were pure and upright, surely now He would awake for you, and prosper your rightful dwelling place. Though your beginning was small, yet your latter end would increase abundantly" (Job 8:5–7).

Has anyone ever tried to give you any advice? It turns out that the one who is giving the advice should apply it first. Several times in my life, people have come to me to give me advice. However, the advice was not of God but the enemy. On one occasion, I encouraged the person to apply the advice to himself.

Bildad spoke wise words, yet those were more for Bildad. Yet God did this for Job. God took all of Job's misfortunes and multiplied them into pure goodness. After Job prayed for his friends, God multiplied all he had lost. "Now the Lord blessed the latter days of Job more than his beginning" (Job 42:12).

Misfortune was never the intended plan for Job, but it was the intended plan of the devil. The latter end of Job did increase abundantly. Job experienced the God of multiplication in his former days and even more in his latter days. The God of multiplication never left Job, even in his trials. His wife, friends, brothers, and sisters misjudged Job for his loss. God allowed it to test Job.

Is God testing you like Job? We can learn that the God of multiplication can restore what the enemy has tried to steal from you. Like Job, God can multiply the blessings taken from us. God still is a God of multiplication and a God of restoration. Surely, God still takes us from glory to glory. Surely, stay faithful to God in your trials and see the God of multiplication bless you double for all your heartaches and troubles.

A couple of years ago, I was diagnosed with breast cancer. I really did not know what to do. I was in a state of shock. Meanwhile, I was having trouble with my left knee. The doctor inserted a medication into my knee, and it did not work well. It left me with an allergic reaction. I ended up in the hospital for eleven days and ten nights. In the hospital room, I prayed and sang. The doctors even gave me the possibility of amputating my left leg.

I reached out to a dear friend of mine, an evangelist and intercessor, asking him to put me in his prayers. I remember praying and singing at 3:00 a.m., and around 5:00 a.m., I fell asleep. In that situation, the God of multiplication gave me a dream while I was in the hospital, one that I will never forget. I happened to be in a church service. The preacher pointed out to me and told me to come to the front because God had a message for me. When I reached the altar, I lifted up my eyes. The preacher was no longer there, but Jesus was. I saw Jesus in a pure-white, bright gown. The light was so magnificent that I could barely see His face.

Then Jesus reached his hands out to me. I grabbed His hand, and the next thing I knew, we both were flying up into the heavens. He said, "Come up." We were flying at a speed so fast that I cannot tell you how fast we were going. Then I started asking questions, and again, Jesus said, "Come up." Again, we flew into another heavenly dimension and at a great speed. Then we stopped with his arm up, I looked up, and I saw the open heavens.

Then in the dream, I was back in the church, where I was there for a couple of hours in the spirit. When I woke up, God spoke to my heart. He showed me the open heavens to let me know that through the trials, He listened to the prayers of his people. God showed Abraham an open heaven with so many stars that Abraham could not count. For Abraham, this experience was of great significance in his life. Abraham was struggling to believe that God would give him a son. Abraham even suggested Eliezer as the one probably giving him a son.

The stars in the open heaven symbolized Abraham's descendants, yet his circumstance was far from having descendants since Sarah was barren. Today, the God of multiplication is still fulfilling the promise to Abraham. Christians need to realize that the God of multiplication will use our trials to bless us even greater.

After this trial, I started the process of my breast cancer journey. I was devastated because this process is tough. I prayed to God and cried many times. Oftentimes I prayed, declared the word, sang, and rested, but many times I was sad, depressed, and anxious because of the medications' side effects. Yet the God of the multiplication has been there the whole time.

One time, I asked God why I was going through this trial. I even asked, "Is it because I sinned or did something wrong?"

God took me to John 9:2–3, where Jesus healed a man born blind and then received sight.

The disciples asked Jesus, "Rabbi, who sinned, this man or his parents, that he was born blind?"

Nevertheless, Jesus answered, "Neither this man nor his parents sinned, but that the works of God should be revealed in him."

Like Job, like many men and women of God who have experienced loss, trials, troubles, sickness, or misfortunes, the God of the multiplication allows it for a purpose. Through the trials, God gives revelations about Himself and demonstrates His mighty works. God allows those experiences to take us from glory to glory. God has many names. I encourage you to call on the name of God in your situation because there is power in the names of God. Spangler shares fifty-two names of God to demonstrate that even the names of God have power. "Though God's name is holy and powerful, it cannot be involved as a magic formula. Rather, his name becomes powerful whenever it is uttered by men and women who are experiencing their faith in God."[70]You can pray on a specific name of God for your specific situation and see God work on your behalf.

- Abba – Father (Luke 15:20)
- Adonay – Master (Psalm 16:2)
- Alpha Kai Omega – Alpha and Omega (Revelation 22:13)
- Arnion – Lamb Of God (John 1:29)
- Artos Zoes – Bread Of Life (John 6:51)
- Aster Lampros Proinos – Bright Morning Star (Revelation 22:16)
- Basileus Basileon – King Of Kings (Revelation 19:16)
- Didaskalos – Teacher (Mark 12:14)
- Ebed – Servant (Mark 10:45)

[70] Ann Spangler, *The Names of God* (Grand Rapids: Zondervan, 2009), 79.

- Ego Eimi – I Am (Exodus 3:14)
- El Chay – Living God (Jeremiah 10:10)
- El Elyon – God Most High (Daniel 4:34)
- El Olam – The Everlasting God (Genesis 21:33)
- El Roi – The God Who Sees Me (Genesis 16:13)
- El Shadday – God Almighty (Genesis 17:1)
- Elohim - God, Mighty Creator (Genesis 1:1)
- Emmanuel – God With Us (Matthew 1:23)
- Esh Oklah – Consuming Fire (Deuteronomy 4:24)
- Ga'al – Redeemer (Isaiah 44:6)
- Hashem – The Name (1 Kings 8:29)
- Hiereus – Priest (Hebrews 4:14)
- Huios David – Son Of David (Luke 1:32)
- Huios Tou Anthropou – Son Of Man (Matthew 12:8)
- Iatros – Physician (Luke 4:23)
- Iesous Soter – Jesus The Savior (Matthew 1:21)
- Leon Ek Tes Phyles Louda – Lion Of The Tribe of Judah (Revelation 5:5)
- Logos – Word (John 1:14)
- Lord Yahweh (Leviticus 18:2)
- Machseh – Refuge (Psalm 91:2)
- Mashiach – Messiah (Acts 2:36)
- Melek – King (Exodus 15:18)
- Migdal Oz – Strong Power (Proverbs 18:10)
- Miqweh Yisrael – Hope Of Israel (Jeremiah 17:13)
- Nymphios – Bridegroom (Revelation 19:9)
- Philos – Friend (John 15:13)
- Poimen Kalos – Good Shepherd (John 10:11)
- Qedosh Yisrael – Holy One Of Israel (Isaiah 29:19)
- Sar Shalom – Prince Of Peace (Isaiah 9:6)
- Shophet – Judge (Psalm 94:15)
- To Phos tou Kosmou – Light Of The World (John 8:12)
- Yahweh Nissi – The Lord My Banner (Exodus 17:15)
- Yahweh Roi – The Lord Is My Sherpherd (Psalm 23:1)

- Yahweh Rophe – The Lord Who Heals (Exodus 15:26)
- Yahweh Shalom – The Lord Is Peace (Judges 6:24)
- Yahweh Shammah – The Lord Is There (Ezekiel 48:35)
- Yahweh Tsebaoth – The Lord Of Hosts (1 Samuel 17:45)
- Yahweh Tsidqenu – The Lord Of Righteousness (Jeremiah 23:6)
- Yahweh Tsuri – The Lord Is My Rock (Psalm 144:1)
- Yahweh Yireh – The Lord will Provide (Genesis 22:14)
- Yeled – Child (Matthew 2:11)

Chapter 11

Multiplication of Sin

And because lawlessness will abound, the love of
many will grow cold.

—Matthew 24:12

In other versions, the word *abound* here is substituted for multiply,
expand, increased, or spread. The multiplication of sin has been
around since the fall of humankind. Sin entered through one man,
so this means everyone has sinned (Romans 3:23).

Earlier in the book, I utilized Genesis 6:5, where God brings
to attention that wickedness is great on earth. Jesus shared the
signs of the end times, for instance, the multiplication of sin.
There is hardly any respect for God, parents, and the life of others.
Lying is part of conversations that you do not know who is telling
the truth or not. Self-love is a priority for so many people that self-
image has become a god in their lives. Fornication is so common
even in our Christian communities that adultery is no longer
taboo. Today, sin is very much accepted, not realizing that we are
deceiving ourselves. Galatians 6:7 reads, "Do not be deceived,
God is not mocked; for whatever a man sows, that he will also
reap." The television is full of sin-bombarding. The news is full
of stories and consequences of the multiplication of sins such as
robbery, killings, attacks, and so on.

The kingdom of Satan is an orderly one. When the multitudes were following Jesus, Jesus demonstrated that He had the power to cast out demons. The Scribes were falsely accusing Jesus as part of the kingdom of Satan because demons were coming out of people. The Scribes knew that one of the signs of the Messiah is that He has the power against the kingdom of Satan, but the Scribes did not accept Jesus as the Messiah.

Jesus replied to the Scribes, "If a kingdom is divided against itself, that kingdom cannot stand. And if a house is divided against itself, that house cannot stand. And if Satan has risen up against himself, and is divided, he cannot stand, but has an end" (Mark 3:24–26).

Jesus is saying, "If I am part of the kingdom of Satan, then how I have the power to cast out Satan?" Jesus is telling the Scribes, "You people got everything figured out wrong."

Satan is a copier. In heaven, he learned that the God of gods is an orderly God and has an orderly kingdom. God even has meetings (Job 1:6). God has a hierarchy set in place: God, seraphim, cherubs, archangels, angels, and creatures unknown to humans. Satan is a fallen angel. His name means enemy or adversary, and he is a deceiver. Wanting to be like God, Lucifer and one-third of the angels rebelled against God. God overthrew him and his followers. Satan fell like lightning from heaven (Luke 10:18). This was the start of his kingdom. Other names for Satan are:

- Abaddon (Psalm 88:11)
- Leviathan (Job 41:1)
- Dragon (Job 41:1–34; Revelation 12:3–4, 7–9)
- Lawless One (2 Thessalonians 2:8–10)
- Power of Darkness (Colossians 1:13)
- Prince of the Power of Air (Ephesians 2:2)
- Antichrist (1 John 2:18, 22)
- Liar (1 John 2:22)

- Beelzebub (Mark 3:22)
- Devil (Matthew 4:1)
- Tempter (Matthew 4:3; 1 Thessalonians 3:5)
- A God of This Age (2 Corinthians 4:4)
- Adversary, Enemy (1 Peter 5:8)
- Ruler of the Darkness (Ephesians 6:12)
- Father of Lies, Murderer (John 8:44)
- Abyss, Bottomless Pit, Apollyon, King of the Bottomless Pit (Revelation 9:11)
- Thief (John 10:10)
- Transforms as an Angel of Light (2 Corinthians 11:14)
- Leads the Word Astray (Revelation 12:9)
- Accuser of Our Brethren (Revelation 12:10)
- Beast (Revelation 13:2)
- Belial (Deuteronomy 13:13, 2 Corinthians 6:15)
- Evil One (Matthew 13:19)
- Lucifer/Day Star (Isaiah 14:12)
- Ruler of This World (John 14:30)
- Son of Perdition (John 17:12)
- Serpent of Old (Revelation 20:2)
- Fallen Star (Isaiah 14:12–14)

Paul wrote to the Ephesians and gave them a clear view of how the dominion of Satan operates here on earth. Look at Ephesians 6:12, "For we do not wrestle against flesh and blood, but against principalities, against powers, against the rulers of the darkness of this age, against spiritual hosts of wickedness in the heavenly places."

The hierarchy of Satan is in the air. God gave humankind dominion of the earth, but through sin, Adam gave authorization for Satan to operate his kingdom here on earth. This is why the darkness of powers operates here on earth. There are ranks in the kingdom of Satan, principalities (states ruled by the prince of darkness), and powers delegated by Satan for specific purposes, rulers over dominions, and spiritual hosts that are demons, unclean spirits, or evil spirits.

Satan's organized kingdom is real. A great example is in Daniel 9–10, when Daniel prayed and fasted for twenty-one days. From the first day that Daniel proposed to seek God, God listened and sent an answer, but there was opposition. The kingdom of darkness sent the prince of the kingdom of Persia to intervene in Gabriel, delivering the message to Daniel that Michael came to help in this battle. The goal of Satan is to steal, kill, and destroy through the multiplication of sin. People sin because of ignorance, unknowingly or knowingly. Sinning is a choice. Sin calls out for another sin because one sin needs another sin to cover the first sin. Easily, this is how sin can multiply. For example, if someone wants to lie, that person has the power to lie, but for sure, another sin must appear to cover the lie.

Ananias and his wife decided to lie in regard to what portion to give to God. One lie calls another lie. Both agreed on the lie to deceive the man of God, but in reality, they were deceiving themselves. The lies of Ananias and Sapphira led to their own death. Yet if the person is doing it unknowingly or knowingly, sinning brings consequences, for instance, on a personal, family, community, and even national level.

Personal or private sin is deadly. Just because it is private does not mean that the spiritual world is not seeing. This includes the kingdom of God and the kingdom of Satan. Proverbs 5:21–23 says, "For the ways of man are before the eyes of the Lord, and He ponders all his paths. His own iniquities entrap the wicked man, and he is caught in the cords of his sin. He shall die for lack of instruction, and in the greatness of his folly he shall go astray." Er, son of Judah, was wicked before God, and God killed him. Then his brother, Onan, needed to do the right thing, to give an heir to his brother, Er, but he selfishly and privately did not do the right thing. This displeased God, and God killed him.

It is in the heart that sins come forth. The devil knows who is upright or not. The sons of Sceva tried to exorcise those who had evil spirits. The evil spirits answered back at them, "Jesus I know, and Paul I know, who are you" (Acts 19:15). What power do you have if you do not fast, pray, read the Word, and live an upright life? How can you expect to affect the lives of others if there are sins?

Sin has destroyed families in the past and present, and it will continue in the future. Achan decided to steal. Then he hid the stolen items in his tent. Even Israel lost a battle due to the sin of Achan. Tragically, Achan and his whole family were stoned and burned. It only takes one family member to act upon sinful desires to jeopardize a family. Today, families are under attack continuously. The value or respect of family is not the same as it used to be years ago. The concept of what a family constitutes is questioned not only in our legal system but also in Christian communities. It only took one sin to enter the world and to see the product of sin still multiplying today, affecting not only individuals and families but also nations.

Due to their sins, Israel and Judah went to captivity. The consequences of sins can bring a nation down to its knees until the nation recognizes where it has fallen. The multiplication of sins is in each nation. One cannot say I am going to move to this nation because there is no sin there. The reality is that sin is everywhere. It has multiplied itself into the cities to remote areas of the earth. Like a plague, sin has taken over. Sin causes spiritual, intellectual, and physical damage. This is why the Bible is full of stories of people who not only sinned but also how their lives were changed. Leprosy entered into the life of Gehazi through the sin of greed. Numbers 32:23 says, "Take note, you have sinned against the Lord; and be sure your sin will find you out."

Sin opens the doors for demons to come in. Demons demonstrate the power of sin. One demon will go find another demon to help him out in keeping the person tied or bound to the sins. Demons can travel to different locations and oppress people in different places or countries. This is why many times, it is so difficult for many people to let go of pornography, fornication, adultery, stealing, gossiping, and so forth. Only the power of Jesus can liberate people under demonic influences. Demonic possession is real. Through Jesus's ministry, many were set free.

On one occasion, Jesus was teaching in the synagogue, and a man with an unclean spirit cried out, "Let us alone" (Mark 1:24). Here, the unclean spirit is referring to self as "us," meaning there was more than one unclean spirit. On another occasion, the demons spoke and told Jesus that Legion was their name because they were many unclean spirits. Unclean spirits working together tried to destroy the life of this man by tormenting him.

On one occasion at a Sunday service, a woman was in the midst of the crowd, but no one knew she was possessed. The man of God started preaching, and out of nowhere, the possessed woman started emitting loud voices. Interrupting the service, the man of God rebuked the demons, but the demons shook her, that she ran out of the church toward the street for the purpose of killing her. The ushers brought the woman back into the church. She was liberated from those tormenting unclean spirits that were telling her to kill herself. You should have seen the before and after because this woman was transformed and displayed the joy of the Lord openly.

God is still in the business of liberating people who are oppressed by demonic forces. People enter the church and leave exactly as they came possessed, tormented by unclean spirits because the church lacks what the primitive church had, the demonstration of power. How can we preach about Jesus without the demonstration of power? The primitive church was able to liberate so many people who were in sin and oppressed by the enemy because they received power (Acts 1:8).

In writing to the Romans, Paul reminded them, "Where sin abounded, grace abounded much more, so that as sin reigned in death, even so, grace might reign through righteousness to eternal life through Jesus Christ our Lord" (Romans 5:21). Paul acknowledged the inevitable abounded sin is a reality, but through Christ Jesus, grace abounds more exceedingly. Jesus gives us the overflow of grace. This is where sin has failed that it cannot surpass the overflow of grace.

Chapter 12

Defending Christianity

> And out of the ground the Lord God made every tree grow that is pleasant to the sight and good for food. The tree of life was also in the midst of the garden, and the tree of the knowledge of good and evil.
>
> —Genesis 2:9

As I was sleeping, I had a dream in which I was sitting, and someone else was sitting beside me, but I could not tell who this person was. Nor could I see the teacher's face. The teacher was like an angel. He was in a white gown, and a brilliant light emanated from him. Yet, I was in deep thought absorbing the material. I saw a tree in front of me. In my spirit, it was revealed that this was the Tree of Knowledge of Good and Evil. Right in front of the tree was a blackboard where the teacher was explaining the material.

The problem of evil originated from the Tree of Knowledge of Good and Evil. Even though there were other trees, the Tree of Knowledge of Good and Evil was specifically prohibited by God. God spoke to Adam, instructing him not to eat of this fruit because surely he would die. This meant spiritual and physical death. This restriction from God made the Tree of Knowledge of Good and Evil different from the other trees. Without the knowledge of evil, sin would have been unknown since sin is the action of doing evil.

The power of multiplication was already in effect in the garden of Eden. We see this in the creation, where God saw that everything was good. The earth brought forth grass, the herb that yields seed according to its kind, and the tree that yields fruit, whose seed is in itself according to its kind. The animals were reproducing.

However, there was no knowledge of evil nor the multiplication of evil but only the multiplication of pure goodness. The fact that the power of multiplication has its history in the Creator denotes that Christianity holds the truth. Yes, the power of multiplication derives from God the Creator, but the multiplication of evil came into the world through a choice of disobedience, which was in the Tree of Knowledge of Good and Evil. The power of multiplication testifies that we live in a God-created world. The power of multiplication confirms that we live in a world where good and evil as well as angels and demons exist and people reap what they sow.

Adam was the first to receive the instruction in regards to the Tree of Knowledge of Good and Evil. Then God created Eve because it was not good for man to be alone. Adam told Eve not to eat or touch the fruit. Satan appeared in the garden as a serpent. When the astute serpent came to Eve, she was alone. Satan, knowing about the restriction, bombarded Eve with questions, "Has God indeed said, 'You shall not eat of every tree of the garden'" (Genesis 3:1).

This is the main strategy that the world utilizes against Christianity. The world bombards Christianity with questions such as: Is there actually a God? Is there a God that really created the earth and the heavens? Is there actually a God that allows suffering?

David says, "The fool has said in his heart, 'There is no God.' They are corrupt, they have done abominable works, there is none who does good" (Psalm 14:1). Christians from all over the world are bombarded with these typical questions, so Christians like Eve will question themselves if they are on the right path.

Eve quickly reminded Satan that she was not supposed to eat or touch it because surely she would die. This did not stop Satan from replying hastily, "You will not surely die" (Genesis 3:4). Here, Satan is challenging Eve with what God says. Atheists are not afraid to challenge Christians with what the Word of God says because they reject the idea that there is the existence of God. To accept the existence of God, then the Bible is true, so there is a hell. Peter reminded the church to "but sanctify the Lord God in your hearts, and always be ready to give a defense to everyone who asks you a reason for the hope that is in you, with meekness and fear" (1 Peter 3:15).

When the temptation came to Eve, she really was misled by a false appearance by the only deceiver, the devil. Eve was not equipped, but today the church has no excuses. Christians should be equipped to defend the God of the power of multiplication because, in Him, we hold the truth of the gospel. In defending the gospel, Christians must uphold an attitude of meekness with humility and patience.

The serpent continued telling Eve, "For God knows that in the day you eat of it your eyes will be opened, and you will be like God, knowing good and evil" (Genesis 3:5). The devil presented his argument with half a truth and the other half with a lie. The devil was saying to Eve, "You will not die, but you will be like God, knowing good and evil." This statement became false because God commanded the man, saying, "Of every tree of the garden you may freely eat; but of the tree of the knowledge of good and evil you shall not eat, for in the day that you eat of it you shall surely die" (Genesis 2:16–17).

When the serpent presented his false arguments to Eve, according to Smith, the devil was challenging the justice of God.[71]

---

[71] Chuck Smith, *C2000 Series on Genesis 2–3*, https://www.blueletterbible. org/Comm/smith_chuck/c2000_Gen/Gen_002.cfm.

Here are some examples of how the world bombards Christianity with challenges about the justice of God: what good God would allow children to have cancer? Alternatively, what good God would send people to hell?

The unbeliever asks questions because they do not understand the things of God because the unbeliever chooses not to believe that the Bible holds the truth. Isaiah 30:18 says, "For the Lord is a God of justice." Even Paul reminded the church of Corinth, "But the natural man does not receive the things of the Spirit of God, for they are foolishness to him; nor can he know them, because they are spiritually discerned" (1 Corinthians 2:14).

The atheists and even secular humanists want to understand the problem of evil from the perspective of the natural man, but to be able to understand the problem of evil, it is crucial to accept the things of God so He may reveal the truth to them.

When Eve touched the fruit, she realized that she did not die, so that led her to bend her elbow and bring the fruit to her mouth. In agreement with Smith, "So he (the devil) hit her (Eve) with a three-pronged attack with the lust of the flesh, the lust of the eye, and pride of life (1 John 2:16)."[72] Again, Adam and Eve were already experiencing the power of multiplication of goodness in their life. They lacked nothing but had it all. On the other hand, Adam was not deceived like Eve; rather, "Adam knew what he was doing. Adam's was a deliberate, willful choice against God's command."[73] Both of their eyes were opened, and both hid from God's presence.

God did not create humankind to be like a robot, but rather every man and woman has a free will to choose to obey God or to give their backs to Him. It is a choice that every individual here on earth makes. Because of Adam and Eve's disobedience, their relationship with God was broken. Now their open eyes could no longer just see the power of multiplication of the goodness of

---

[72] Ibid.
[73] Ibid.

God, but now the power of multiplication of evil was present in their lives. Even when they entered their new world, the power of multiplication of good and evil followed them.

In Genesis, God revealed Himself as a God of justice when He deliberately gave a sentence first to the serpent, then to the woman, and finally to Adam (Genesis 3:14–19). It was an authoritative decision that God remarked, "The man has become like one of Us, to know good and evil" (Genesis 3:22). For those who do not believe in the Trinity God, here is another verse that proves the truth that the Father God, the Son, and the Holy Spirit are present in the creation.

Christianity has the answers that the world is looking for in regards to the problem of evil. The origin of the multiplication of evil being experienced today originated in the garden of Eden when both Adam and Eve made a choice to listen to Satan, accept the temptation, and choose to eat the forbidden fruit. While they were in the eastward side of the garden of Eden, they experienced the freedom of the multiplication of goodness, but they had one rule, to abstain from eating from the Tree of Knowledge of Evil and Good.

God placed the Tree of Knowledge of Good and Evil and the Tree of Life in the midst of the garden. God wants His children to walk in His freedom. This includes accepting and walking under His rules. God gave the Ten Commandments that are as valid today as when He gave them to Moses on Mt. Sinai. Jesus gave a new commandment to "love your neighbor as thyself." The church, walking in the freedom of God, takes responsibility to follow these commandments. In doing these, the power of multiplication demonstrates itself in pure goodness. Even though the church will experience afflictions or hardships, God will turn them to work for the good of His people.

In defending the gospel, the church must be ready to answer for the world the questions that they feel need to answer. Here the church can utilize this tool to preach the gospel. Jesus commanded

His disciples to "go into all the world and preach the gospel to every creature (Mark 16:15). This includes those worldviews that challenge the church with questions that may seem hard for many Christians, but for others maybe not. The church must become literate or be knowledgeable in the Word.

One of the challenges that the church is facing today is that Christians are not reading their Bible and are raising a generation that is illiterate to the Word of God. How can the church stand against different worldviews of today if it becomes increasingly illiterate? Geisler states, "Of the three major worldviews, atheism affirms the reality of evil and denies the reality of God. Pantheism affirms the reality of God but denies the reality of evil. Theism affirms the reality of both God and evil."[74]

Evil exists. It is real, and there is a story behind the problem of evil that Christianity holds the truth. The world has a big void; the church cannot fill it. Only God can, but through the church, we can influence the world by bringing the Word of God into the light to the world. The church should be able to be ready to answer questions related to the Word of God and our worldview.

After Adam and Eve were cast out of the garden of Eden, their lives were never the same. In Genesis, God started the history of humanity with a couple, while in Revelation Jesus returned for the church, the bride. Adam waited for Eve to be created and given to Him. Today, the church is supposed to be ready and ready for her husband.

However, is the church ready to be lifted? Is the church doing what it is supposed to be doing? Is the church giving the right answers to a world that needs Jesus? How can a good God exist while there is evil in the world? Where did evil come from? Is there a God? Why is there suffering? To be ready to answer such questions is to preach and defend the gospel.

---

[74] Norman L. Geisler, *The Big Book of Christian Apologetics* (Grand Rapids, Mich.: BakerBooks, 2012), 139.

Conclusion

> Therefore, my beloved brethren, be steadfast, immovable, always abounding in the work of the Lord, knowing that your labor is not in vain in the Lord.
>
> —1 Corinthians 15:58

For the power of multiplication to manifest in our lives, we have to put in the work. Faith plus hard work equals the power of multiplication. God has given us the power of multiplication, but many do not realize it is there for either good or evil. God wants to show us His glory. God wants His people to increase in the knowledge of His Word. God is willing to help us grow more each day in Him. We have to pay the price. We all have a calling, but we have to work at it. Besides being responsible and living an orderly life before God and humankind, we have to take the time to pray, fast and meditate on His Word. There we will find more truth about the power that has given us to multiply. Not only does God want to bless our finances and multiply them, but He also wants us to multiply in grace and favor of our jobs, family, friends, community, or nation.

Even more, as Christians, we need to demonstrate to the world the power of multiplication but the goodness of God. God wants to multiply in us more love, peace, and joy so we may reflect to the world that Jesus is the way to salvation. God wants us to multiply in us more glory and strength and seek Him profoundly. The more we seek Him, the more God wants to multiply more of His blessings upon us, so we are a blessing to others.

Currently, there is a hunger in the world to see the power of multiplication of the goodness of God. There is so much hunger to see miracles, supernatural, and glory of God that many do not know how to get it. Let me tell you: God wants to show you and me more of the power of multiplication. Still, in these times, we must live an orderly Christian life. Our lives must be in order. We must obey God and His commandments. We must be an example everywhere we go because we represent Jesus here on earth. We must be responsible in every area of our lives, including in our jobs and with our family, our bills, and everything else. We must work hard to be intimate with God each day. We must give our tithes and offerings to Him. As God used you to give advice or counsel to others, apply that advice to you too. Be an example.

Jesus multiplied the fishes and loaves of bread. People knew He had the power of multiplication because the word of God was in Him. He led by example. Jesus always took time to pray and fast, and when Jesus spoke, He only spoke the word of God. Jesus meditated on the word of God daily. Jesus blessed. Jesus blessed the bread and the fish. Bless your job, your family, your circumstance, your health, the area where you live, and your neighbor. Pray and bless your enemies. Blessings are a powerful tool given to us Christians to see more of God's goodness upon our lives.

In Matthew 15:35, we see Jesus is active in His ministry. People followed Jesus for three days, and miracles happened around Him. Jesus is the formula that many are looking for. Through Jesus, we can obtain the power of multiplication for things to be manifested in our lives. Jesus had compassion for the people because they were hungry not only physically but also spiritually.

In the world, many are walking hungry, and we Christians

have the answer for them. We must have compassion for others. We have to move more in a spirit of compassion so others will know and even experience the power of multiplication in God. Jesus took the loaves of bread and the fish and gave thanks to God. A thankful heart moves God in your favor. A thankful heart is so powerful that it touches God's heart. A thankful heart believing that the power of multiplication is still available to us today can bring about great results.

After giving thanks, the power of multiplication said, "Now I AM doing the work." After you give thanks for what you have right now and for what you are asking for, then God is going to show you the power of multiplication being manifested in the now of your life, but you have to believe. 3 John 1:2 says, "Beloved, I pray that you may prosper in all things and be in health, just as your soul prospers."

God wants all of us in Christ to prosper. When talking here about prosperity and multiplication, I am talking about any area of your life that God wants to take you to another level. He wants to see your life in that power given to us to multiply and become fruitful so we may be blessings to others. I encourage you to keep moving and working. If God is calling you to the ministry, God will confirm and open the doors for you to walk in. If you want more peace, love, or joy, or if you lack faith, God today wants to multiply that. Keep fighting the good fight. Do not give up. In Him, Christ Jesus, we are more than conquerors, and the power of multiplication is ours. The enemy wants to think that you do not have it, but in Christ Jesus, we are more than conquerors.

Bibliography

Abbott-Smith, G. *A Manual Greek Lexicon of the New Testament.* New York: Charles Scribner's Sons, 1922.

Anders, Max, and Gary Inrig. *Holman Old Testament Commentary.* Nashville: Broadman & Holman Publishers, 2003.

Barry, J. D., et al. *Faithlife Study Bible.* Bellingham: Lexham Press, 2012.

Beale, G. K. *1 -2 Thessalonians The IVP New Testament Commentary Series.* Downers Grove: IVP Academic, 2003.

Benson, Michael T. *Harry S. Truman.* Westport: Praeger Publishers, 1997.

Blue Letter Bible. 2018. https://www.blueletterbible.org/ (accessed 2018).

Brackman, Rabbi Levi, and Sam Jaffe. *Jewish Wisdom for Business Success Lessons from the Torah and Other Ancient Texts.* New York: American Management Association, 2008.

Cole, R. Alan. *Exodus An Introduction and Commentary Tyndale Old Testament Commentaries Volume 2 .* Downers Grove: IVP Academic, 1973.

—. *Mark Tyndale New Testament Commentaries Volume 2.* Downers Grove: IVP Academic, 1989.

Dictionary.com. 1995. https://www.dictionary.com/ (accessed 2015).

Dockrey, Karen, Johnnie Godwin, and Phyllis Godwin. *The Student Bible Dictionary*. Uhrichsville: Barbour Publishing, 2000.

Geisler, Norman L. . *The Big Book of Christian Apologetics*. Grand Rapids: BakerBooks, 2012.

Grypeou, Emmanouela, and Helen Spurling. *The Book of Genesis in Late Antiquity: Encounters Between Jewish and Christian Exegesis*. London and Boston: Brill, 2013.

Hagee, John. *In Defense of Israel*. Lake Mary: Frontline A Strang Company, 2008.

Hamilton, Victor P. *Exodus An Exegetical Commentary*. Grand Rapids: Baker Academic, 2011.

Heiser, Michael S. *The English-Hebrew Reverse Interlinear Old Testament New King James Version*. Bellingham: Lexham Press, 2009.

Kartje, John. *Wisdom Epistemology in the Psalter A Study of Psalms 1, 73, 90, and 107*. Berlin and Boston: De Gruyter, 2014.

Lea, Thomas D., and David Alan Black. *The New Testament Its Background and Message 2nd Edition*. Nashville: B & H Academic, 2003.

Lennox, John C. *Joseph: A Story of Love, Hate, Slavery, Power, and Forgiveness*. Wheaton: Crossway, 2019.

Longman III, Tremper. *Tyndale Old Testament Commentaries Volumes 15-16 Psalms*. Downers Grove: IVP Academic, 2014.

Longman, Tremper III. *Jeremiah Lamentations Understanding the Bible Commentary Series*. Grand Rapids: Baker Books, 2008.

Luck, Steve. *American Desk Encyclopedia*. New York: Oxford University Press, Inc., 1998.

Martin, Glen S. *Holman Old Testament Commentary Exodus, Leviticus, Numbers*. Nashville: Broadman & Holman Publishers, 2002.

McCraw, Thomas K. *The Founders and Finance*. Cambridge: The Belina P Press of Harvard University Press, 2012.

Oden, Thomas C. *Ancient Christian Commentary on Scripture Old Testament I Genesis 1-11*. Chicago and London: Fitzroy Dearborn Publishers, 2001.

Peer, Andrea. *Global poverty: Facts, FAQs, and how to help*. November 21, 2018. https://www.worldvision.org/sponsorship-news-stories/global-poverty-facts (accessed September 18, 2019).

Petterson, Anthony R. *Haggai, Zechariah & Malachi Apollos Old Testament Commentary*. Downers Grove: IVP Academic, 2015.

Purcell, Aaron D. *Deal and the Great Deppression*. Kent: The Kent State University Press, 2014.

Radmacher, Earl, Ron Allen, and H. Wayne House. *Compact Bible Commentary*. Nashville: Thomas Nelson, 2004.

Roden, Chet. *30 Days to Genesis A Devotional Commentary*. Timmonsville: Seed Publishing Group, LLC, 2016.

—. *Elementary Biblical Hebrew An Introduction to the Language and Its History*. San Diego: Cognella, 2017.

Schreiner, Thomas R. *Romans Baker Exegetical Commentary of the New Testament*. Grand Rapids: Baker Academic, 1998.

Smith, Chuck. "C2000 Series on Genesis 2-3." *Chuck Smith :: C2000 Series on Genesis 2-3*. Blue Letter Bible, 1979 - 1982.

Spangler, Ann. *The Names of God*. Grand Rapids: Zondervan, 2009.

Stevenson, Kenneth, Michael Glerup, Thomas C. Oden, and C. Thomas McCollough. *Ancient Christian Commentary on Scripture Old Testament XII Ezekiel, Daniel*. Downers Grove: IVP Academic, 2008.

Stiefel, Barry L. *Jewish Sanctuary in the Atlantic World A Social and Architectual History*. Columbia: University of South Carolina Press, 2014.

Taylor, Richard A., and E. Ray Clendenen. *The New American Commentary Haggai, Malachi Vol 21A*. Nashville: B & H Publishing Group, 2004.

Vos, J. G. *Genesis.* Pittsburgh: Crown & Covenant Publications, 2006.

Wenham, Gordon J. *Numbers An Introduction and Commentary.* Downers Grove: IVP Academic, 1981.

Winship, A. E. *Jukes-Edwards A Study in Education and Heredity.* Harrisburg: R. L. Myers & Co., 2005.

Zacharias, Ravi. *I, Isaac, take Thee Rebekah.* Nashville: Thomas Nelson, 2004.

Printed in the United States
by Baker & Taylor Publisher Services